Developing Tests and Questionnaires for a National Assessment of Educational Achievement

National Assessments of Educational Achievement

VOLUME 2

Developing Tests and Questionnaires for a National Assessment of Educational Achievement

Prue Anderson and George Morgan

**Vincent Greaney and
Thomas Kellaghan, Series Editors**

 **THE WORLD BANK**

1818 H Street NW
Washington DC 20433
Telephone: 202-473-1000
Internet: www.worldbank.org
E-mail: feedback@worldbank.org

Cover design: Naylor Design, Washington, DC

ISBN: 978-0-8213-7497-9
eISBN: 978-0-8213-7498-6
DOI: 10.1596/978-0-8213-7497-9

Library of Congress Cataloging-in-Publication Data
Anderson, Prue, 1954–
  Developing tests and questionnaires for a national assessment of educational achievement / Prue Anderson, George Morgan.
    p. cm.—(National assessment of educational achievement ; volume 2)
  Includes bibliographical references and index.
  ISBN 978-0-8213-7497-9 (alk. paper)—ISBN 978-0-8213-7498-6
  1. Educational tests and measurements—United States. 2. Educational evaluation—United States. I. Morgan, George, 1945– II. Title.
  LB3051.A715 2008
  371.26'1—dc22
                                                                2008002684

CONTENTS

PREFACE   xi

ABOUT THE AUTHORS AND EDITORS   xiii

ACKNOWLEDGMENTS   xv

ABBREVIATIONS   xvii

PART 1   CONSTRUCTING ACHIEVEMENT TESTS

CHAPTER 1   INTRODUCTION   3

CHAPTER 2   DEVELOPING AN ASSESSMENT FRAMEWORK   9
                The Test Blueprint or Table of Specifications 10
                Validity   16
                Test Language   16
                Item Format   17
                Student Population to Be Assessed   24
                Reporting Results   24
                Contexts   25

CHAPTER 3   ITEM WRITING   27
                Item Difficulty   29
                Item Bias   30
                Stimulus Material   30
                Item Format   33
                Practice Items   45

	Item Layout and Design	46
	The Item-Writing Team	52
	Item Panels	55
	Other Reviewers	57
	Tracking Items	58
CHAPTER 4	**PRETESTING ITEMS**	**61**
	Designing the Pretest Form	64
	Printing and Proofreading the Pretest	68
	Implementing the Pretest	70
	Scoring the Pretest	71
	Reliability	76
CHAPTER 5	**SELECTING TEST ITEMS**	**79**
CHAPTER 6	**PRODUCING THE FINAL TEST**	**85**
	Designing the Final Test	85
	Printing and Proofreading	88
CHAPTER 7	**HAND-SCORING TEST ITEMS**	**91**
PART 2	**CONSTRUCTING QUESTIONNAIRES**	**97**
CHAPTER 8	**DESIGNING QUESTIONNAIRES**	**99**
	Questionnaire Content	102
	Questionnaire Blueprint	105
	Questionnaire Items	105
	Item Format	108
	Language of the Questionnaire	109
	Respondents	109
	Questionnaire Administration	110
	Data Analysis Plan	111
CHAPTER 9	**ITEM WRITING FOR QUESTIONNAIRES**	**113**
	Questions	114
	Statements	114
	Response Categories	115
	Managing Sensitive Issues	117
	Questionnaire Layout	117
	Reviewing Questionnaires	119
CHAPTER 10	**CODING QUESTIONNAIRE RESPONSES**	**121**
	Preparing Questionnaires for Data Entry	123
	Coding Missing or Ambiguous Responses	123

CHAPTER 11	MATCHING QUESTIONNAIRES AND TEST DATA	125
	Student Questionnaires	125
	Parent Questionnaires	126
	Teacher and Head-Teacher Questionnaires	126
PART 3	DESIGNING A MANUAL FOR TEST ADMINISTRATION	127
CHAPTER 12	THE TEST ADMINISTRATORS' MANUAL	129
	Contents of the Manual	130
	Use of the Manual	131
	Features of a Manual	132
	How Much Detail Is Necessary?	132
	Practice Questions	134
	Tryout	134
	Review	137
CHAPTER 13	THE TEST ADMINISTRATOR	139
	Choice of Test Administrator	139
	Following Instructions	140
	Quality Assurance	142
	Administrator's Checklist	142
CHAPTER 14	INFORMING SCHOOLS ABOUT THE NATIONAL ASSESSMENT	145
APPENDIX A	GLOSSARY	147
APPENDIX B	FURTHER READING	153
APPENDIX C	EXAMPLES OF TEST AND QUESTIONNAIRE ITEMS AND ADMINISTRATION MANUALS ON CD	157
INDEX		163

BOXES

2.1	Papua New Guinea Mathematics Curriculum	11
2.2	New Zealand English Curriculum	11
2.3	Examples of Multiple-Choice Items	18
2.4	Example of a Closed Constructed-Response Item	19
2.5	Examples of Open-Ended Short-Response Items	19

2.6	Example of an Essay Prompt	20
3.1	Example of Irrelevant Stimulus Material	32
3.2	Example of an Item with Inaccurate or Misleading Information	33
3.3	Example of a Multiple-Choice Item	34
3.4	Punctuation in Complete Sentences	35
3.5	Punctuation in a List	35
3.6	Minimizing Reading	36
3.7	Item with a Negative Stem	36
3.8	Poorly Paired Distractors	37
3.9	Dealing with Pairs in Distractors	37
3.10	Confusing Open-Ended Item with Unclear Directions	40
3.11	Good Example of a Closed Constructed-Response Item	41
3.12	Item with Partial Credit	42
3.13	Example of an Open-Ended Response Item with Scoring Guide	43
3.14	Example of a Closed-Constructed Item with Scoring Guide	44
3.15	Using Pictures to Reduce Words	48
3.16	Keeping Images Simple	49
3.17	Labeling Graphs Clearly	49
3.18	Labeling Maps Clearly	50
3.19	Leaving Space in the Stimulus Material	51
3.20	Example of Style Sheet for Item Writers	54
4.1	Example of an Item in Multiple-Choice and Open-Ended Format	71
4.2	Example of a Data Entry Sheet for a Pretest	73
6.1	Example of a Test Cover Page	86
8.1	Attitudes and Values Questionnaire Blueprint	106
9.1	Poor Alignment of Boxes and Response Categories	118
9.2	Better Alignment of Boxes and Response Categories	118
10.1	Grayscale Coding Example	122
10.2	Example Treating Items as Separate Categories for Data Entry	122
12.1	Administration Manual Instructions	133
12.2	Information for Teachers and Principals	134
12.3	Administration of Practice Items	135
13.1	Administration Checklist: An Example from the Philippines	143

FIGURES

1.1	National Assessment Organizational Chart	4
1.2	Overview of National Assessment Activities	5
4.1	Example of Circular Linking of Items	65
4.2	Model for Vertically Linking Items	66
C.1	Guide to CD Materials on Tests, Questionnaires, and Manuals	158

TABLES

1.1	National Assessment Stages in Test Development and Questionnaire Design	6
2.1	Blueprint for a Middle Primary Mathematics Test	13
2.2	TIMSS Mathematics Blueprint, Grades 3 and 4	14
2.3	Papua New Guinea Mathematics Content Blueprint	15
2.4	Advantages and Limitations of Item Formats	23
2.5	Papua New Guinea Mathematics Test-Item Formats	24
4.1	Link Items in Two Reading Units	67
4.2	Part of a Spreadsheet for Tracking Items across Forms	68
5.1	Example of Output from Analysis of a Multiple-Choice Item	80
5.2	Example of Output from Analysis of an Open-Ended Partial-Credit Item	81
8.1	Components of Questionnaire Development	101
8.2	Functions of Reading in an International Study: Weights Used to Create Two New Variables, "Reading for a Utilitarian Purpose" and "Reading for Enjoyment"	107

PREFACE

The quality of any educational assessment exercise depends on the quality of the instruments used. In fact, if these instruments are poorly designed, the assessment can be a waste of time and money. *Developing Tests and Questionnaires for a National Assessment of Educational Achievement*, the second of five books in the *National Assessments of Educational Achievement* series, describes how to develop technically robust instruments for a national assessment of educational achievement, with a particular focus on carrying out this task in developing countries. Volume 1 in the series describes the key purposes and features of national assessments and is mainly aimed at policy makers and decision makers in education. This second book and most of the subsequent books in the series provide step-by-step details on the design, implementation, analysis, and reporting of a national assessment and are intended primarily for national assessment teams.

Developing Tests and Questionnaires for a National Assessment of Educational Achievement addresses the design of two types of data collection instruments: student achievement tests and background questionnaires. Part 1 covers the development of an assessment framework and a test blueprint, item writing, pretesting, and final test layout. Part 2 delineates comparable stages and activities in the construction of background questionnaires, which are used to gather information from students, teachers, head teachers, or parents on variables that might help explain differences in student performance on the achievement test. Part 3 describes how to design a manual for test administration to help ensure that all students take the test under standardized conditions. The compact disc (CD) that accompanies this book offers examples of well-designed test items, questionnaire items, and administration manuals drawn from national and international assessments and is meant to showcase the variety of ways in which assessment teams have approached the design of these instruments.

Volume 3 in the series focuses on practical issues to be addressed in implementing a large-scale national assessment program, including logistics, sampling, and data cleaning and management. Volume 4 deals with how to generate data on items and test scores and how to relate the test scores to other educational factors. Finally, volume 5 covers how to write reports that are based on the national assessment findings and how to use the results to improve the quality of educational policy making.

As readers make their way through this volume, it should become evident that the development of assessment instruments is a complex and time-consuming exercise that requires considerable knowledge, skill, and resources. At the same time, experience has shown that the payoff from well-designed instruments can be substantial in terms of the quality of the information provided on levels of student achievement and on school and nonschool factors that might help raise those achievement levels. Good-quality instruments can increase the confidence of policy makers and other stakeholders in the findings. They also can increase the likelihood that policy makers will use the results of the national assessment to develop sound plans and programs designed to enhance educational quality. If the test and questionnaire results achieve these outcomes, they will more than justify the time and effort involved in their development.

Marguerite Clarke
Senior Education Specialist
The World Bank

ABOUT THE AUTHORS AND EDITORS

AUTHORS

Prue Anderson is a senior research fellow at the Australian Council for Educational Research. She has developed reading assessment materials for system-level testing programs for primary and lower secondary students She has worked on educational monitoring programs in Australia, Brunei Darussalam, Papua New Guinea, and the Philippines. Currently, she is project manager of the International Schools' Assessment program. Other areas of professional interest include (a) mapping assessment data against curriculum outcome statements and frameworks and (b) measuring social outcomes of schooling.

George Morgan is an educational consultant. He was a senior research fellow in the Measurement Division and head of the Mathematics and Science Test Development Group at the Australian Council for Educational Research for almost 30 years. He has developed mathematics and science curriculum and assessment materials across all educational levels and has worked on large-scale testing programs. More recently, he has been closely involved with assessment projects in Cambodia, East Timor, the Lao People's Democratic Republic, Papua New Guinea, and Samoa.

EDITORS

Vincent Greaney is an educational consultant. He was lead education specialist at the World Bank and worked in a range of countries in Africa, Asia, and the Middle East. A former teacher; a research fellow at the Educational Research Centre at St. Patrick's College, Dublin; and a visiting Fulbright professor at Western Michigan University, Kalamazoo, he is a member of the International Reading Association's Reading Hall of Fame. Areas of interest include assessment, teacher education, reading, and promotion of social cohesion through text-book reform.

Thomas Kellaghan is director of the Educational Research Centre at St. Patrick's College, Dublin, and is a fellow of the International Academy of Education. He has worked at the University of Ibadan in Nigeria and at the Queen's University in Belfast. Areas of research interest include assessments and examinations, educational disadvantage, and home-school relationships. He served as president of the International Association for Educational Assessment from 1997 to 2001. He has worked on assessment issues in Africa, Asia, Latin America, and Middle East.

ACKNOWLEDGMENTS

A team led by Vincent Greaney (consultant, Human Development Network, Education Group, World Bank) and Thomas Kellaghan (Educational Research Centre, St. Patrick's College, Dublin) prepared the series of books titled *National Assessments of Educational Achievement*, of which this is the second volume. Other contributors to the series include Sylvia Acana (Uganda National Examinations Board), Prue Anderson (Australian Council for Educational Research), Fernando Cartwright (Canadian Council on Learning), Jean Dumais (Statistics Canada), Chris Freeman (Australian Council for Educational Research), Hew Gough (Statistics Canada), Sara Howie (University of Pretoria), George Morgan (Australian Council for Educational Research), T. Scott Murray (UNESCO Institute for Statistics), and Gerry Shiel (Educational Research Centre, St. Patrick's College, Dublin). The work was carried out under the general direction of Ruth Kagia, director of education, and Robin Horn, manager, Human Development Network, Education Group, both at the World Bank. Robert Prouty initiated the project and managed it up to August 2007. Marguerite Clarke managed the project in its later stages through review and publication.

We are grateful for contributions of the review panel: Al Beaton (Boston College), Irwin Kirsch (Educational Testing Service), and Benoit Millot (World Bank). Additional helpful comments were provided by Helen Abadzi, Regina Bendokat, Marguerite Clarke,

Robin Horn, Elizabeth King, Maureen Lewis, Harry Patrinos, Carlos Rojas, Jee-Peng Tan, Eduardo Velez, and Raisa Venalainen.

We received valuable input and support from Carly Cheevers, David Harding, Aidan Mulkeen, Aleksandra Sawicka, Thi Tran, Hilary Walshe, and Hans Wagemaker.

We wish to thank the following institutions for permission to reproduce material in the text and in the accompanying compact disc: Australian Council for Educational Research; Educational Research Centre, Dublin; International Association for the Evaluation of Educational Achievement; Massachusetts Department of Education; National Center for Education Statistics of the U.S. Department of Education; Organisation for Economic Co-operation and Development; and the Papua New Guinea Department of Education.

Book design, editing, and production were coordinated by Mary Fisk and Paola Scalabrin of the World Bank's Office of the Publisher.

The Irish Educational Trust Fund, the Bank Netherlands Partnership Program, the Educational Research Centre, Dublin, and the Australian Council for Educational Research have generously supported preparation and publication of the series.

ABBREVIATIONS

CD	compact disc
CTT	classical test theory
ID	identification number
IRT	item response theory
MOE	ministry of education
NAEP	U.S. National Assessment of Educational Progress
NSC	national steering committee
PIRLS	Progress in International Reading Literacy Study
PISA	Programme for International Student Assessment
SDS	senior district supervisor
STBA	student test booklet allocation
TIMSS	Third International Mathematics and Science Study or Trends in International Mathematics and Science Study

PART 1

CONSTRUCTING ACHIEVEMENT TESTS

1

INTRODUCTION

Many activities are involved in a national assessment, from the moment someone decides to carry one out to the moment someone sits down to read a report of its findings. Each book in this series of five volumes, titled *National Assessments of Educational Achievement*, describes some of the activities involved in a national assessment, with particular reference to carrying out such an assessment in developing countries. Much of the technology that is required to carry out a satisfactory national assessment in countries that lack a strong tradition of empirical educational research is unlikely to be available locally. Therefore, an effort has been made in the series to spell out in detail the activities of an assessment and, where relevant, to help readers (who we can assume will have responsibility for at least some aspects of an assessment) understand why the activities are required.

The ministry of education (MOE) or its appointed national steering committee (NSC) will usually have overall responsibility for guiding and supporting a national assessment. Under the supervision of the MOE or NSC, most of the work will be carried out by an implementing agency, which, in turn, will supervise the work of the test development manager, subject specialists, and statistical analysts and will be responsible for the logistical arrangements for running the national assessment. This book, *Developing Tests and Questionnaires for a*

National Assessment of Educational Achievement, covers mainly the activities of the test development manager and subject specialists, as well as pretesting arrangements (see figure 1.1). Other topics shown in figure 1.1, such as sampling; logistical aspects of assessment, including contacting schools, and data entry and data cleaning are dealt with in volume 3 of this series, *Implementing a National Assessment of Educational Achievement*. Volume 4, *Analyzing Data from a National Assessment of Educational Achievement*, covers statistical analysis.

The flowchart depicted in figure 1.2 summarizes the various steps in a national assessment. Many of the steps are described in this book; the shaded boxes or activities relate to the aspects of the assessment that receive most attention in this book. The book also features a number of pointers or comments common to more than one aspect of assessment; these have been repeated to facilitate reader interested in a single aspect of national assessment.

FIGURE 1.1

National Assessment Organizational Chart

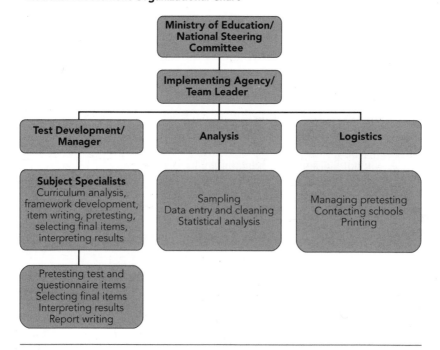

Source: Author's representation.

FIGURE 1.2

Overview of National Assessment Activities

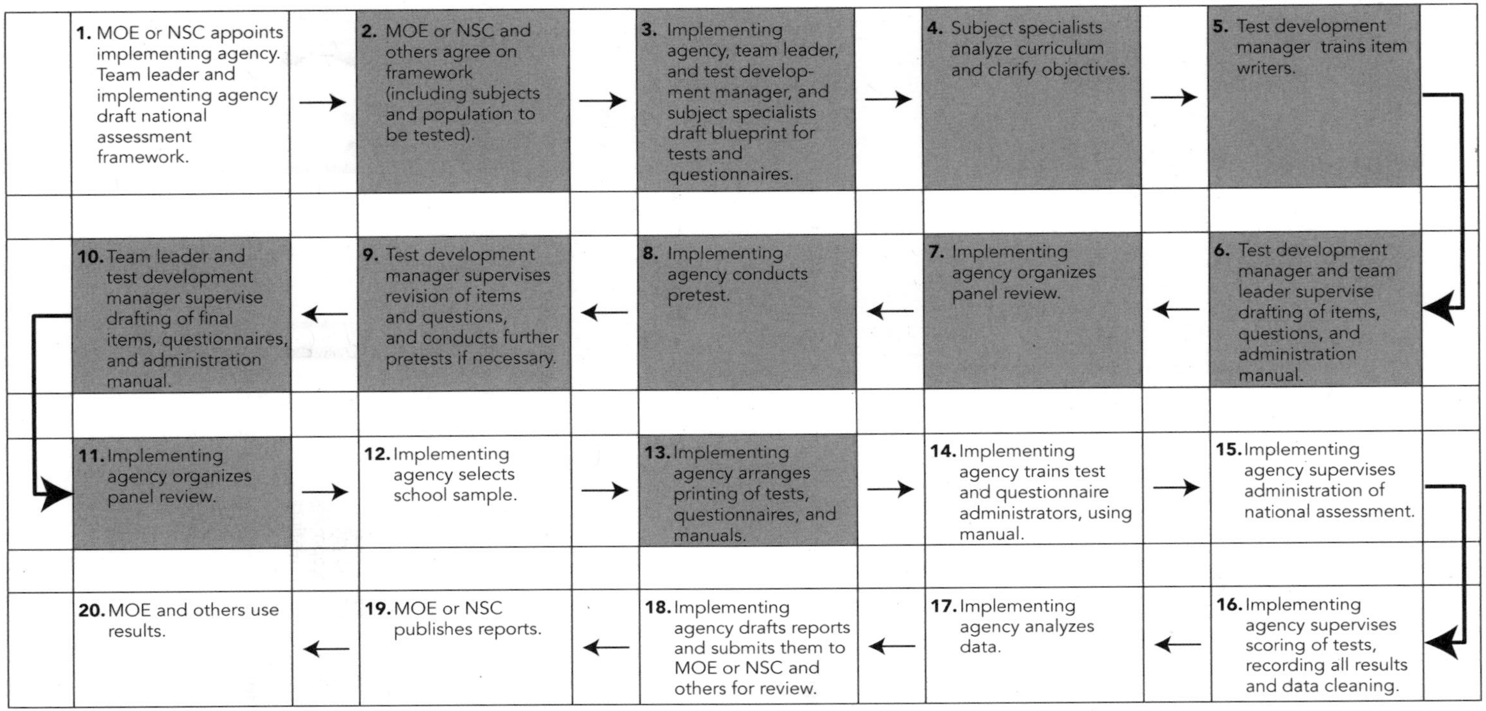

1. MOE or NSC appoints implementing agency. Team leader and implementing agency draft national assessment framework.

2. MOE or NSC and others agree on framework (including subjects and population to be tested).

3. Implementing agency, team leader, and test development manager, and subject specialists draft blueprint for tests and questionnaires.

4. Subject specialists analyze curriculum and clarify objectives.

5. Test development manager trains item writers.

6. Test development manager and team leader supervise drafting of items, questions, and administration manual.

7. Implementing agency organizes panel review.

8. Implementing agency conducts pretest.

9. Test development manager supervises revision of items and questions, and conducts further pretests if necessary.

10. Team leader and test development manager supervise drafting of final items, questionnaires, and administration manual.

11. Implementing agency organizes panel review.

12. Implementing agency selects school sample.

13. Implementing agency arranges printing of tests, questionnaires, and manuals.

14. Implementing agency trains test and questionnaire administrators, using manual.

15. Implementing agency supervises administration of national assessment.

16. Implementing agency supervises scoring of tests, recording all results and data cleaning.

17. Implementing agency analyzes data.

18. Implementing agency drafts reports and submits them to MOE or NSC and others for review.

19. MOE or NSC publishes reports.

20. MOE and others use results.

Source: Authors.

TABLE 1.1

National Assessment Stages in Test Development and Questionnaire Design

Stage	Activity	Approximate time	People involved
1	Prepare assessment framework; clarify the purpose of the national assessment, tests, and questionnaires; and select population.	4 weeks	MOE or NSC, and implementing agency, especially team leader, test development manager, key stakeholders, and policy makers
	Design the blueprint, or table of specifications, and consult widely for approval.	4 to 6 weeks	MOE or NSC, implementing agency, test development manager, expert groups, experienced teachers, subject specialists, data analysts, experienced item writers, key stakeholders, and policy makers
2	Write test and questionnaire items.[a]	12 to 14 weeks (20 to 30 items per writer per week)	Test development manager, subject specialists, item writers, and key stakeholders
	Produce pretests and draft questionnaires.	4 weeks	Team leader, test development manager, item writers, design and layout professionals, and proofreaders
	Print pretests and draft questionnaires.	2 weeks	Implementing agency, team leader, test development manager, and item writers
	Pack and distribute pretests and draft questionnaires.	2 to 3 weeks	Implementing agency
3	Administer pretests and draft questionnaires in schools.	2 to 3 weeks	Implementing agency and test administrators
	Hand-score items (if required).	2 weeks	Team leader, test development manager, subject specialists, and item writers
	Enter pretest data.	1 week	Implementing agency data analyst and data entry personnel

	Task	Time	Personnel
4	Analyze pretest and questionnaire data.	2 weeks	Implementing agency, data analyst, item writers, and test development manager
	Select items for tests and questionnaires.	2 weeks	Test development manager, analysts, item writers, and key stakeholders
5	Produce final tests, questionnaires, and administration manuals.	2 weeks	Implementing agency, test development manager, design and layout professionals, proofreaders, and item writers
	Print tests and questionnaires.	4 weeks	Implementing agency, team leader, and test development manager
	Pack and distribute tests and questionnaires.	2 to 3 weeks (depending on distance and accessibility)	Implementing agency and test development manager
6	Administer tests and questionnaires in schools.	3 to 4 weeks	Implementing agency, test development manager, and test administrators
	Hand-score items (if required).	3 to 4 weeks	Test development manager and item writers
7	Enter and clean data.	4 to 6 weeks	Data analyst and data entry personnel
	Analyze data.	2 to 3 weeks	Data analyst, item writers, and test development manager
8	Produce final reports.	4 to 5 weeks	Data analyst, item writers, and test development manager

Source: Authors.
a. Additional time will be required if items have to be translated into other languages.

Additional related information on test development and questionnaire design is provided in table 1.1. The table describes the process of constructing achievement tests and questionnaires in terms of eight stages and also indicates the individuals responsible for the components.

The compact disc (CD) that accompanies this book features many examples of test items, questionnaire items, and test administration manuals. Further details on the contents of the CD are given in appendix C. This material, drawn from national and international assessments, is presented to familiarize national assessment teams with items and item types in a number of curriculum areas and with questionnaires designed for students, teachers, schools or principals, and parents.

DEVELOPING AN ASSESSMENT FRAMEWORK

An assessment framework that provides an overall outline or plan to guide the development of assessment tests, questionnaires, and procedures is crucial in determining the contents of an assessment (Linn and Dunbar 1992; Mullis and others 2006). Such a framework helps provide a good understanding of the construct (for example, achievement in reading or mathematics) that is being assessed and the various processes that are associated with that construct. It should include a definition of what is being assessed, identify the characteristics of the tasks that are going to be used in developing the test, and provide a basis for interpreting the results (Kirsch 2001; Messick 1987). A framework can help explain the purpose of an assessment. It can facilitate discussion and decision making among educational stakeholders by clarifying key concepts before the assessment commences. The framework can also identify key variables likely to be associated with the test score and can help ensure that these variables are included in the design of the national assessment.

At the outset, the steering committee should agree on a definition of what is to be measured. In many instances, the national curriculum document will contain definitions of key subject areas. Definitions of reading, for example, have varied over time and across education systems. In some instances, reading has been equated with the ability to pronounce words. In others, reading refers to the ability to identify individual words and give their meaning. Reading has also been defined as the ability to comprehend or get meaning from a text. More recent definitions go beyond simple decoding skills and include the ability to use information from texts as well as to develop an understanding of them. They also recognize that students and adults read for a variety of purposes, such as for enjoyment or for information. These new definitions are reflected in tests that include different forms of texts, such as short stories, excerpts from newspapers, advertisements, signs, and charts.

The purpose for which data will be collected must be clear in test development. Early consultation with key stakeholders and expert groups is a critical first step in clarifying the purpose of a national assessment and, consequently, what the test should assess, who should be assessed, when they should be assessed, and in what language the tests should be given. Curriculum experts should be involved in these decisions, as well as policy makers and education managers, who will be in a position to use the results of the assessment as a basis for educational policy, allocation of resources, and implementation of reforms.

National assessments can be powerful tools for evaluating the effectiveness of some aspects of the curriculum. Well-designed assessments can also reinforce curriculum intentions by modeling the kinds of skills and understandings students should be able to demonstrate. These kinds of skills and the contexts in which they are assessed should work together to support overarching policy aims of education in key learning areas. The examples of some overarching contexts for national assessments in boxes 2.1 and 2.2 reflect a number of educational priorities.

THE TEST BLUEPRINT OR TABLE OF SPECIFICATIONS

The test blueprint, or table of specifications, is the critical document that guides test development, analysis, and report writing. It describes the data that must be collected, defines the test length, and specifies

BOX 2.1

Papua New Guinea Mathematics Curriculum

The 2003 Papua New Guinea elementary cultural mathematics curriculum has the following overarching rationale:

> All citizens have the right to participate in the future development of Papua New Guinea. For this reason, students need to develop sound mathematical knowledge, skills, and understanding.... Students at Elementary [level] will be able to link new mathematical concepts from the five strands in this syllabus to their existing cultural knowledge so that they can confidently use mathematics in their everyday lives. The Elementary Cultural Mathematics course provides many opportunities for relevant and purposeful learning that is built on the principles of home life. (Papua New Guinea, Department of Education 2003: 2)

The focus of this rationale (along with ministerial policy documents and a substantial restructuring of primary and preprimary education) is to embed primary mathematics in the village culture of the students. Reforms have placed priority on the integration of primary mathematics with the local culture and the application of mathematical understandings to everyday life. A recent national assessment developed to monitor student achievement emphasized using realistic contexts for questions and assessing skills and understandings that have practical applications.

BOX 2.2

New Zealand English Curriculum

The general aims of the New Zealand English curriculum state:

> Students should be able to: engage with and enjoy language in all its varieties [and] understand, respond to, and use oral, written, and visual language effectively in a range of contexts. (New Zealand, Ministry of Education 2002: 9)

These aims highlight the importance of interest and pleasure in reading and understanding a wide variety of texts. Engaging texts and meaningful enjoyable tasks are key considerations in system-level assessments of English. The emphasis on language in all its varieties reflects a strong commitment to recognizing and valuing the oral language culture of the Maori students as well as the written forms of English. Various national assessments reflect these aims.

the proportion of items in a test that will address the various aspects of a curriculum. A good blueprint should indicate the following:

- The proportion of test items in the final form that address each curriculum area (for example, mathematics, language, science)
- The proportion of items within a curriculum area that assess different skills (for example, in mathematics—number, measurement, space, and pattern; in writing—ideas, content knowledge, structure, style, vocabulary, spelling, and grammar)
- The proportion of items that address different cognitive processing skills (such as knowledge or recall, interpretation or reflection)
- The proportion of multiple-choice and open-ended items
- The proportion of items devoted to stimulus texts of different kinds in reading (such as narrative, expository, procedural, and argumentative) or in mathematics (such as tables, charts, and diagrams)

The test blueprint in table 2.1 is based on a mathematics curriculum for the middle grades of primary school. Separate subtests were designed to measure pupils' abilities to carry out basic computations, to understand mathematical concepts, and to solve problems. For example, the cell formed by the intersection of the content area "Fractions" and the intellectual behavior "Ability to solve routine problems" represents the objective "Ability to solve routine problems involving fractions." A committee of subject-matter specialists, which included teachers, decided to devote five items to that objective. The cell that contains items testing the ability to carry out operations with whole numbers received the highest weighting (25 items). Many cells had no items. The relative weights of importance assigned to each objective guided test development and later the compilation of the final version of the test.

The blueprint for mathematics from the Third International Mathematics and Science Study (TIMSS)[1] in table 2.2 defines the item formats and the cognitive processes to be addressed for grades 3 and 4 in a somewhat different way.

Clearly, blueprints vary depending on understandings of the construct being measured and on the purpose of an assessment. Everyone involved in test development should understand and approve the

TABLE 2.1

Blueprint for a Middle Primary Mathematics Test

Content areas	Computation			Intellectual behaviors — Concepts						Problem solving				Overall total
	Knowledge of terms and facts (A1)	Ability to carry out operations (A2)	Total	Under-standing of math concepts (B1)	Under-standing of math principles (B2)	Under-standing of math structure (B3)	Ability to translate elements from one form to another (B4)	Ability to read and interpret graphs and diagrams (B5)	Total	Ability to solve routine problems (C1)	Ability to analyze and make comparisons (C2)	Ability to solve nonroutine problems (C3)	Total	
1. Whole numbers	1	25	26	1	4	7	2	4	18	14	2	2	18	62
2. Fractions		4	4	4	1	2			7	5			5	16
3. Decimals		8	8			5		1	6	5			5	19
4. Measurement	2		2				3	2	5	3			3	10
5. Geometry			0	2	2				4				0	4
6. Charts and graphs			0						0		4		4	4
Overall total	3	37	40	7	7	14	5	7	40	27	6	2	35	115

Source: Educational Research Centre 1978: 44.

TABLE 2.2

TIMSS Mathematics Blueprint, Grades 3 and 4

Performance expectations	Total number of items[a]	Multiple-choice items	Short-answer items	Extended-response items
Knowing	42	35	7	0
Performing routine procedures	16	13	3	0
Using complex procedures	24	21	2	1
Solving problems	20	10	3	7

Source: IEA, http://timss.bc.edu/timss1995i/TIMSSPDF/AMitems.pdf.

a. The number of items reflects the total item pool that was used to form 26 test clusters in eight different test booklets. No student was required to take the full test.

implications of a blueprint in terms of what should be tested and what should be left out.

Because of limitations of time and resources, it is not possible to test every substrand of a curriculum area or all the topics that are covered in a syllabus. Test items should always address core skills. Curriculum or subject experts should be consulted to determine which skills are core.

The importance given in the national assessment blueprint to substrands or domains of a curriculum also depends on the way the test data will be reported (by overall score or by curriculum domain). Educational policy makers should be consulted to find out how they would like the test data reported.

If the test data will be reported as a single overall score for each student in a curriculum area, such as mathematics, then at least 25 or 30 items are required. Data on a somewhat smaller number of items may be required to report on a substrand, such as students' understanding of space or problem solving, in a mathematics test.

Table 2.3 provides an example of a content table of specifications for a mathematics test for students in grades 3, 5, and 8 in Papua New Guinea. Note that in the grade 3 test, more than 80 percent of the items cover number and application, space and shape, and measurement. Only four items address chance and patterns. By grade 8, the items are spread more evenly across each of the substrands.

Blueprints are usually based on a prescribed (or intended) curriculum. However, if the implemented curriculum (what teachers teach) and the achieved curriculum (what students have learned) are not

TABLE 2.3

Papua New Guinea Mathematics Content Blueprint

Grade	Number and application	Space and shape	Measurement	Chance	Patterns and algebra[a]	Total items
Grade 3	10	7	4	2	2	25
Grade 5	10	10	7	4	4	35
Grade 8	10	10	8	6	6	40

Source: Unpublished material from the Papua New Guinea Department of Education.
a. Algebra applies only to grade 8.

taken into consideration, a test may be too hard or too easy. Hence, it will not provide a meaningful description of the range of student achievements in the target population. If most students fail to answer items correctly, the test does not show whether these students are able to demonstrate skills that are just below or well below the level of difficulty of the items in the test. Similarly, if most students answer all the items correctly, the test does not indicate whether they are capable of demonstrating skills that are just above or well above the difficulty of the items in the test. Data from tests that are too hard or too easy are of limited use to policy makers, schools, or teachers.

The difficulty of the test depends on its purpose. If the purpose is to monitor the performance of all students in the target population, then the distribution of difficulty of the test items should match the distribution of achievement of the target population. As a general rule, two-thirds of the test should consist of items that two-thirds of the population have between a 30 and 70 percent likelihood of answering correctly. (On average, the likelihood should be 50 percent to help maximize the variation in student test scores.) The other third of the test should be evenly divided between items that more than 70 percent of students taking the test are likely to answer correctly and items that fewer than 30 percent are likely to answer correctly. Although sensitivity to the student achievements that these figures reflect is important, it should not lead to the exclusion of important areas of the curriculum simply because students perform very poorly or very well on them. The suitability of items should be established in a pretesting program in which items are administered to students with characteristics similar to those in the target population for the national assessment.

Some national assessments set achievement or performance levels that are based on a preset standard and identify students who have met this standard. If the standard is very high, the test will identify the small number of students who demonstrate this level of skill, but it will give little information about the level of achievement of the rest of the population other than that the level is below the standard. If the standard is low, the test will identify the large number of students who demonstrate this level of skill, but it will give little information about any higher levels of skills these students might also have acquired.

VALIDITY

Validity is a broad construct that involves making appropriate interpretations and uses of scores or test information (Messick 1989). One facet of validity is the extent to which the content of a test is representative of the curriculum or construct that is being measured. The test development manager is responsible for coordinating with a nominated reference group of subject specialists, such as curriculum specialists, to ensure that the items represent an adequate sampling of a curriculum or construct. The expert group should not include the item writers. In this instance, validity is a judgmental, not a statistical, issue. The expert group should determine if the test represents an adequate coverage of a specified subject (such as grade 4 mathematics) and should consider if performance on the test provides adequate evidence of student achievement in the subject area.

TEST LANGUAGE

The test framework should clarify and justify the language or languages to be used in the national assessment tests. The language of a test is usually the medium of instruction. Translating test items in cases where instruction occurs in multiple languages tends to be costly and time consuming. Translated versions of tests need to be as equivalent as possible if the data are to be used for comparative purposes. The following are some issues to consider in deciding to test a particular curriculum area using one or more than one language.

- Assessing older students in a common language of instruction may be preferable if resources are limited.
- Reducing the words used in test items to a bare minimum can reduce translation costs, but it also typically decontextualizes the item, thereby making it less authentic.
- Excluding some students from the target population in the national assessment may be preferable to attempting to accommodate all linguistic groups.
- Sometimes the intended language of instruction is not the actual language used in teaching. In such instances, the items in the national assessment test might use the actual language of instruction.
- In the case of younger students, especially if the language of instruction is not the first language, the test can be administered orally. The test administrator reads each question aloud or plays it on a tape recorder and gives students sufficient time to respond. This form of assistance can be particularly appropriate for tests of mathematics and science administered to younger students, who may be able to demonstrate a greater degree of subject mastery on an orally administered test than on a test that requires them to read the test items independently. Tests designed to assess students' independent reading skills, of course, should not be administered orally.

ITEM FORMAT

In paper-and-pen assessments, students respond to a series of questions or prompts. Their written or drawn responses are used as evidence of their level of knowledge, competence, or understanding. There are four basic item formats, or ways that students can show their responses:

- Multiple choice
- Closed constructed response
- Open-ended short response
- Essay or extended response

BOX 2.3

Examples of Multiple-Choice Items

1. Which of these would be most likely to be measured in milliliters?

   A. The amount of liquid in a teaspoon

   B. The weight (mass) of a pin

   C. The amount of gasoline in a tank

   D. The thickness of 10 sheets of paper

Source: IEA 1998, sample item.
Note: A is the correct answer.

2. A bottle of apple juice costs $1.95. Bread costs $2.75. Which of these is the smallest amount you need to buy the apple juice and the bread?

   O $3.75   O $4.00   O $4.80   O $5.00

Source: Australian Council for Educational Research n.d., sample item.
Note: $4.80 is the correct answer.

Multiple-choice items (see box 2.3) require students to select one of several (usually four) options. Options may be written out or shown as labeled pictures. They may be listed one under the other, shown as a horizontal row, or given in two columns. Students indicate their response by shading a bubble, drawing a ring around an alphabet letter or number, or ticking a box to select a piece of text or a diagram. Multiple-choice items have one unequivocally "correct" option and several plausible but incorrect options. The accompanying compact disc (CD) contains many examples of multiple-choice items in language, mathematics, and science for primary- and postprimary-level students.

Closed constructed-response items (see box 2.4) have one correct answer that the student generates. Minor variations in the way the answer is shown are usually acceptable. Students may be required to write one or two words, underline a word or number in a text or table, draw a line on a grid, or indicate an area of a diagram. Closed constructed-response items may also require students to select several options that meet certain criteria or to match a series of pairs of sentences or diagrams. (See, for instance, CD items 6, 9, 11, and 19 on the *NAEP Mathematics Test 1990–2000 for Grade 4* and items S011032 and S031053 on the *TIMSS 2003 Grade 4 Science Test.*)

BOX 2.4

Example of a Closed Constructed-Response Item

Here is a number sentence:

$2,000 + \boxed{} + 30 + 9 = 2,739$

What number goes where the $\boxed{}$ is to make the sentence true?

Answer: _____

Source: IEA 1998, sample item.

BOX 2.5

Examples of Open-Ended Short-Response Items

a. How can you find out how old a tree is after it is cut?

_____

_____

b. Write down one example of how machines help people do their work.

_____

_____

Source: IEA 1998, sample item.

Open-ended short-response items (see box 2.5) require students to generate a response for which several different but correct answers may exist. Usually, the correct response requires some explanation, the demonstration of a process, or a detailed drawing (more than one or two lines). It may require the student to write one or two sentences; complete a series of steps or equations; or complete several aspects of a graph, chart, or diagram. (See, for instance, CD items 6, 7, and 11 in "Appendix B: Dolphin Rescue," *Reading International Grade 4 PIRLS 2006 Sample Items.*)

Essay or extended-response items (see box 2.6) require students to develop a lengthy, sometimes complex, response to a prompt. The response can comprise one or more pages of text, possibly including diagrams. There are many "correct" ways to respond in an essay or extended response. (See, for instance, CD question 9, "A Just Judge," *Reading International PISA 2000 Reading Items,* and items 33, 35, and 39 in *NAEP Main Reading, 1990–2006: Grades 4.*)

BOX 2.6

Example of an Essay Prompt

Essay prompts may be written or illustrated. It is important that the students understand what kind of writing they are being asked to do. For example, students may be asked to explain their ideas, express an opinion, write a persuasive piece, or write a story. This information is usually provided as part of the test administration instructions.

The picture prompt shown in the following example was used in Papua New Guinea to assess students' language skills in writing a narrative story. The test administrator told the students that they could use the ideas in the picture or think of their own ideas for a story about hunting.

Write a story about going hunting.

Source: Papua New Guinea Department of Education 2004.

The first three item formats are most commonly used in national assessments, partly because of the cost of reliably hand-scoring large numbers of essays. The test framework document should indicate the estimated percentages of different item types in the final test. It should also include samples of item types to help members of the steering committee and other stakeholders become familiar with the assessment approach.

The choice of item format and the way the items are scored significantly affect the overall cost of the test. Items that require hand-scoring cost more and take more time, thereby delaying publication of a report. Hand-scoring guides have to be developed, and raters must be employed and trained. The more complex the scoring guides, the greater the costs. Essays and extended-response items tend to cost most. Multiple-choice items cost less to score but are more expensive than other item types to construct. Some cost issues to consider in selecting the item formats for the test are outlined below.

Multiple-choice items are usually scored as correct or incorrect by the data analysis software. It is not necessary to score the items before analysis. It is only necessary to enter the students' responses into a computer. These responses are either entered electronically through scanning or entered manually. Scanning is most economical for large-scale testing. It requires special equipment and sometimes technical backup support. Scanned items may be restricted to a particular response format (such as shading bubbles). A wider variety of multiple-choice styles (such as drawing circles around words, ticking boxes, or drawing lines to select options) can be used if data entry is done manually.

Multiple-choice items should not simply be scored as correct or incorrect before data analysis. Valuable diagnostic information about student performance can be obtained by recording each option. If data are being scanned, one must ensure that all responses are recorded. The cost of manual data entry for multiple-choice items is reduced by the use of consistent layout.

Closed constructed-response items must be hand-scored because a number of different responses may be acceptable. The scoring guides should specify the range of acceptable and unacceptable answers. Usually, the range of possible correct options for closed constructed-response items is limited. Scoring guides are relatively straightforward, and rater training time can be reasonably brief, but quality controls need to be implemented and maintained.

Open-ended short-response items are hand-scored. The number and range of acceptable and unacceptable responses can be large. Hence, scoring guides may be quite complex and may require careful rater training. Ongoing cross-checking during rating is essential for quality control.

Extended-response items have complex scoring guides, and extensive rater training is required. Ongoing double-rating of some or all scripts during scoring is essential for quality control. The scoring guides also require extensive elaboration for training purposes. They should include examples of responses matching each of the levels of the scoring guide.

Different item formats can be combined in the same test. For example, a test may consist of some multiple-choice items, some closed constructed-response items, and some open-ended short-response items.

Item writers should try to ensure that the format of each test item is an appropriate and efficient way to assess understanding of a particular learning outcome. They should also try to minimize the amount of unnecessary reading, writing, or calculating required in answering a particular item.

Decisions about which format or formats to use in a test and what proportion to use them in should be based both on the appropriateness of the format to measure a construct or area of knowledge or skill and on practical constraints, such as the expertise required to develop different item formats and the cost of hand-scoring. Table 2.4 summarizes some advantages and limitations of item formats.

The Papua New Guinea mathematics tests vary the ratio of multiple-choice to open-ended short-response questions, depending on the grade being assessed (see table 2.5). Grade 8 has more items than grade 3. Most of this increase is taken up by more open-ended short-response items.

The amount of time students are given to do a test should be sufficient to allow most students to attempt most items. Collecting information about the amount of time students take to do the pre-test or field-testing items is important. Tests vary in length, but students should be able to attempt the vast majority of the items in about 40 minutes. Tests with mainly multiple-choice items may have more items than tests with mainly short-response items. Tests for secondary students may include more items, and students may be given more time to do the test. If students are unfamiliar with the item formats in an assessment, they are likely to need more time to respond to the items.

TABLE 2.4

Advantages and Limitations of Item Formats

Item format	Advantages	Limitations
Multiple choice	• Many items in one test can address a wide range of outcomes. • Items can make fine distinctions in students' knowledge and understanding. • Hand-scoring is not required, so testing is relatively inexpensive.	• Expertise is required to develop high-quality items. • Students do not generate understanding. • Students may guess.
Closed constructed response (one- or two-word answer)	• Students locate or recall information themselves. • Hand-scoring is relatively straightforward.	• Items usually address a limited range of outcomes (mainly retrieval and recall).
Open-ended short response (one- or two-sentence answer)	• Students can be required to generate high levels of understanding. • Items can address a range of outcomes. • Partial understandings can sometimes be measured.	• Expertise is required to write clearly focused items. • Trained raters and quality control measures are required, thus contributing to costs. • Items that take time for students to answer reduce the range of outcomes that can be addressed.
Essay or extended response	• Students can demonstrate a depth of understanding. • A range of partial understandings can be measured.	• A limited range of outcomes can be addressed. • Trained raters and quality control measures are required, resulting in higher costs.

Source: Authors.

TABLE 2.5

Papua New Guinea Mathematics Test-Item Formats

Grade level	Multiple choice	Open-ended short response
Grade 3	20	5
Grade 5	25	10
Grade 8	25	15

Source: Papua New Guinea Department of Education 2004.

STUDENT POPULATION TO BE ASSESSED

The test framework document should define the target population for the assessment (for example, grade 4) and should indicate why this particular population was selected. In a particular country, the framework document could, for instance, justify selecting grade 3 on the grounds that after grade 3 considerable school dropout occurred; it could justify testing of grade 4 because most students should be able to read by that grade; or it could justify testing during the final grade of primary school to assess the learning achievements of students at this important point in the education system. The framework document might also specify subpopulations of students that might be excluded from the national sample, such as students with special educational needs or students in small schools in very remote areas.

REPORTING RESULTS

From the outset, agreement should be reached with the steering committee on how the results should be reported. Ireland's National Assessment of English Reading reported separate scores related to text type and cognitive process. Its assessment framework document proposed assessing two text-type scales (literary and informational) and two process scales (retrieval and inference-interpretation) for grade 1. At the grade 5 level, it proposed assessing three text-type subscales (literary, information-continuous, and information-noncontinuous) and three process scales (retrieval, inference, and interpretation-evaluation) (Eivers and others 2005). The International Adult Literacy Survey used noncontinuous texts to assess performance on the document scale. The framework for the Progress in International Reading Literacy Study (PIRLS) specified that it would scale test items for two reading purposes: reading for literary experience and reading to acquire and use information. It also proposed combining both scales and giving an overall reading literacy score (Campbell and others 2001).

The steering committee should be informed that reporting results by subscales depends on the results of the analysis of items. International assessments and many national assessments use item response modeling to determine whether the test items adequately fit the subscales. At this stage, the steering committee might be given a nontechnical introduction to the concept of reporting results by levels of achievement, commonly referred to as *proficiency levels*, and be asked for its members' views as to the preferred form of test reporting. Student performance could be described in terms of percentage of items answered correctly or in terms of levels such as *advanced* (exceeds the expected standard), *proficient* (meets the expected standard), *basic* (does not meet the expected standard), or *below basic* (performs below the basic level). The number of proficiency levels might have to be revised as a result of pretest and final test analysis. Volume 4 in this series, *Analyzing Data from a National Assessment of Educational Achievement*, covers both item response theory and proficiency levels.

The framework should also indicate the types of national assessment reports to be published at the end of the assessment. These reports might include a technical report; a series of summary reports for specific audiences, such as teacher trainers, curriculum bodies, and policy makers; and press releases and briefings.

CONTEXTS

Many educational policy makers use national assessments to gather additional contextual information about factors that can directly affect or influence the quality of student learning in particular curriculum areas. The steering committee should give general guidance in selecting the contextual variables that should be assessed. That information, in turn, can be used by the implementing agency to guide questionnaire development. Contextual information can be of particular use to policy makers as they attempt to understand reasons for differences in students' levels of achievement.

Many assessments focus on home and school contexts. Home factors typically include socioeconomic status, sometimes measured in terms of home possessions, parental level of education, language spoken in the home, family structure and size, availability of academic guidance, home processes (such as reading to children and other forms of guidance that encourage learning), and home-school relationships.[2] School contexts frequently cover school and classroom resources, school management and organization, nature and level of teacher training, instructional strategies, and classroom environment. Some assessments gather data on pupils' attitudes toward school and individual subject areas, pupils' interests, and pupils' behaviors (for example, the amount of time spent helping at home, working, or reading for pleasure). The details of how to design and write questionnaire items are covered later in this book, and the CD that accompanies the book contains examples of questionnaire items designed to obtain contextual information from students, parents, teachers, and principals.

NOTES

1. After the third study, this series of studies was described as Trends in International Mathematics and Science Study, and the acronym TIMSS was retained.

2. Note that in some countries, there is an aversion to collecting socioeconomic background data.

CHAPTER 3

ITEM WRITING

This chapter describes the characteristics of good items in a test, the guidelines for writing items, the structuring and organization of items to make a test, and the scoring of items.[1] We also describe the roles of personnel involved in test development— the item writing team and other reviewers, working under the direction of the test development manager.

Bear in mind that the quality of a test depends largely on how clearly the test meets its purpose and on the accuracy with which the items match a well-designed blueprint. Good items are clear, relevant to the curriculum, and focused on one aspect of learning. They provide engaging, genuine tasks that are fair to students of different language and cultural backgrounds.

A good item has the following characteristics:

- It addresses a key learning area.
- It is a constructive and meaningful task.
- It can be mapped back to important characteristics stated in the framework or blueprint documents.
- It is fair.
- It follows central issues in the stimulus, not peripheral or trivial details.

- It clearly tells students what they are required to do.
- It stands alone and does not depend on an understanding that has formed the basis of a previous item.
- If about vocabulary, it is directed at the meaning of the word in the context of the text, rather than on general knowledge.
- It is preferably expressed in positive terms; negatives tend to cause confusion.

Item writers can greatly benefit from examining relevant models of high-quality items. Many test organizations publish sample items on the Internet. Publicly released test items may also be sourced from international tests, such as Trends in International Mathematics and Science Study (TIMSS), Programme for International Student Assessment (PISA), and Progress in International Reading Literacy Study (PIRLS), and national assessments from other countries, such as the U.S. National Assessment of Educational Progress (NAEP). The accompanying compact disc (CD) contains many examples of items from these and other sources. Web addresses are given in appendix B.

Publicly released test items can be used in other tests, provided the content material and the wording of the items are appropriate. This material can be a cheap, useful source of test items. These items (together with answers) are often accessible on the Internet. Therefore, such items should not be used if it is likely that students had access to them before taking the national assessment test. Permission can also be obtained from relevant authorities to use appropriate items from secure tests. This approach can be cheaper than developing items. However, curriculum experts will need to review such items and pretest them for suitability.

Developing expertise in writing items for each of the sections of a blueprint takes time. Item writers should have a common understanding of item terminology and of what items are supposed to measure. To achieve this understanding, they should try to classify each draft item as they develop it, using criteria such as the following:

- Item format (for example, multiple choice, closed constructed, open ended)
- Text type (for a reading test) (for example, narrative, expository)
- Intended grade level (for example, grade 5)

- Learning outcome (for example, addition of two-digit whole numbers or identification of the main idea in a story)
- Cognitive process (for example, knowledge, recall, interpretation, or synthesis).

One cannot always know the level of cognitive processing involved in response to an item. If students are unfamiliar with a process, such as summarizing a paragraph of information, it may require a higher level of processing than if they are accustomed to making summaries.

ITEM DIFFICULTY

Getting the right difficulty level for items is a challenging task for most item writers. In many countries, the content of the intended curriculum is too difficult for most students. As a consequence, item writers often have to draft many items to measure skills that are easier than those listed in intended curricula. For example, mathematics achievement tests designed for grade 5 often include items based on objectives that students should have mastered in grades 3 and 4.

Experienced teachers are more likely than education officials or academics to have a good sense of likely item difficulty levels. However, teacher judgment, while helpful, is not adequate. Pretesting items on samples of students roughly similar to those in the target population is essential for gaining initial objective data on item difficulty levels. It can help avoid the common error of developing tests with items that prove to be much too difficult.

Many factors can make items that the item writer considered simple turn out to be quite difficult. Similarly, some items that were designed to be difficult may be worded or presented in such a way that they may prove to be quite easy. In the case of items that use the multiple-choice format, writers should avoid the following:

- Introducing grammatical or logical cues in the stem and key that point to the correct answer, such as a stem that matches a singular noun with all but one option given as plurals
- Introducing absolute terms, such as "always" or "never," that might rule out some options or point to the correct answer

- Making the correct answer much longer or more detailed than the other options
- Including a key word or phrase from the stimulus material in the correct option but not in the other options
- Setting out options in an illogical order or confusing pattern
- Making options and the key overlap significantly, so that discerning the "best" answer depends on language skills rather than knowledge about what is being tested
- Including questions that can be answered without reference to the stimulus.

In the case of constructed-response formats, developing clear scoring criteria that elicit what the item is intended to measure is important.

ITEM BIAS

Students bring a diversity of cultural knowledge and understanding to a test. They should not be penalized or advantaged by life experiences that are not relevant to the knowledge, skills, and understandings that the test is intended to assess. For example, items about a popular male sport might disadvantage females.

Items can also be biased if they upset some students but not others. Stimulus material should not breach ethical, cultural, or other sensitivities. There should be no chance that some students could be offended, frightened, or upset by the test material. The test development manager should sensitize item writers to various forms of bias. Review panels should be encouraged to look out for test or questionnaire items that might be biased or cause offense. The fourth volume in this series, *Analyzing Data from a National Assessment of Educational Achievement*, features a statistical technique that can be used to help identify biased items at both the pretest and final testing stages.

STIMULUS MATERIAL

The stimulus material provides the context for an item. It may be a piece of text, a diagram, a graph, a table, a map, a chart, or a combination of these.

Most test development begins with the selection or creation of appropriate stimulus material. Reading tests are usually based on extended texts that lend themselves to a series of items or a unit that addresses a range of relevant skills. Mathematics and science tests may include short stimulus material, such as several numbers to be added or an equation to be completed. Mathematics and science items may also include a more complex stimulus, such as a graph, chart, table, or diagram with a series of associated items addressing a range of skills.

The stimulus material should clearly present the main features to be assessed. It should not contain superfluous, repetitive, or unnecessary detail. Good stimulus material has the following characteristics:

- It is substantive and worth examining closely.
- It is likely to be of interest to the target audience.
- It is well written and well designed.
- It is optimally challenging, not too hard or too easy.
- It does not pose spurious challenges.
- It is factually correct.
- It offers opportunity for searching questions.
- It is self-contained.

Where appropriate, providing some context for the stimulus material is important. Context may be provided through a heading or a brief introduction. For example, an extract from a science fiction novel might be introduced as follows: "This piece of writing is from a novel set in the future."

Images should preferably be an intrinsic part of the stimulus material, supplying additional meaning. If images are included simply as decoration, they should not assist students in understanding the text.

Sometimes the stimulus material creates an artificial and unnecessary context for an item. Box 3.1 contains irrelevant material. This item is really about surface area. In real life, Irene would not be concerned about the least amount of paper she would use. In reality, she might need a small amount extra to fold over edges. The most able students could answer this item incorrectly by making allowance for additional paper. The item is better written simply as follows: "The length of one side of a cube is 80 cm. What is the surface area of the cube?"

BOX 3.1

Example of Irrelevant Stimulus Material

Irene will wrap this cube with paper. What is the least amount of wrapping paper she will use?

80 cm

A stimulus that attempts to describe a real-life context should be factually accurate. The information in box 3.2 is probably factually inaccurate. Humans do not usually exhibit the kind of growth pattern shown. Children who tend to be tall usually demonstrate this trait from an early age. If uneven growth patterns are required for the stimulus material, then using plants rather than humans may be preferable for comparative purposes.

Items should be written in the simplest and clearest language possible. The wording should be sufficiently simple so that students can reasonably be expected to be able to read it:

- Avoid difficult vocabulary.
- Avoid long sentences.
- Do not use convoluted sentences.
- Do not use difficult logic.
- Avoid ambiguous or vague questions.
- Avoid double negatives.
- Avoid inconsistency (for example, using different units of measurement in the options or different terms to refer to the same thing).
- Do not use vague wording or unfamiliar terms that are not adequately defined.

BOX 3.2

Example of an Item with Inaccurate or Misleading Information

The graph shows the change in height of Mario and Lita as they grow older.

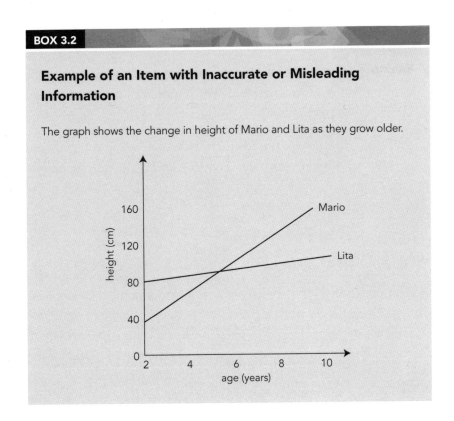

ITEM FORMAT

Two major formats are described: multiple choice and short response (see chapter 2).[2] Consider using a multiple-choice format

- To limit the number of options
- To elicit a succinct answer
- To avoid students having to copy large sections of the stimulus text
- To cover a large range of topics efficiently.

Consider using a short-response format (closed constructed or open ended)

- To test meaning that students must generate for themselves
- To test for different levels of understanding by using a partial-credit item that gives a full score for an answer that shows comprehension of a complex idea and that gives a partial score for an answer that shows comprehension of a simple part of the idea

- To test a restricted and clearly definable range of possible correct responses
- To seek an answer in a situation where the correct answer would be clearly given away in a multiple-choice format because of a lack of plausible incorrect options.

Students should have an adequate command of vocabulary and expression to answer short-answer-type items. Do not use short-response questions if students are likely to copy a large amount of the stimulus text.

Writing Multiple-Choice Items

A multiple-choice item consists of a stem and a number of response options. Sometimes, when a true-false response is required, only two options are required. However, these items are somewhat inefficient. Providing four or five options is more usual. The correct option is the *key*, and the *distractors* are the incorrect options (box 3.3).

The *stem* of an item may take several forms, such as

- An unfinished sentence
- An explicitly stated question
- A sentence containing missing information (Carlos has _____ brothers).

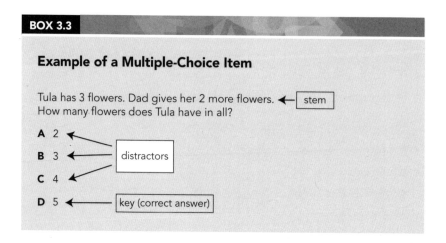

BOX 3.3

Example of a Multiple-Choice Item

Tula has 3 flowers. Dad gives her 2 more flowers. ← stem
How many flowers does Tula have in all?

A 2
B 3 ← distractors
C 4

D 5 ← key (correct answer)

If the stem is an incomplete sentence, it must contain enough information to indicate the nature of the question. The student should not need to read the distractors to infer the question. All the options from an incomplete sentence should

- Be grammatically consistent with the stem
- Be written in a similar style
- Be correctly punctuated
- Start with a lowercase letter and finish with a period.

Remember the following points in writing multiple-choice items:

- *Punctuate complete sentences correctly.* In box 3.4, all the options are complete sentences with the appropriate punctuation.
- *Punctuate lists appropriately.* In box 3.5, the options are lists of words. These options are not punctuated.

BOX 3.4

Punctuation in Complete Sentences

What did Miho think of the market?

A It was crowded, and the food was good.

B It was cheap, and the food was delicious.

C The food was good, but no one was there.

D It was cheap, but the food wasn't very good.

BOX 3.5

Punctuation in a List

How long will Joe stay in Bali at his grandfather's house?

A one week

B two weeks

C one month

D two months

- *Minimize the amount of reading.* To minimize the amount of reading required, the item writer should place as much of the item as possible in the stem (see box 3.6).
- *Avoid negative stems.* Because a negative stem causes confusion, its use should be avoided. If the stem can be expressed only negatively, highlight the word "not" by using bold type or italics (see box 3.7). If a negative stem is unavoidable, the options must never be negative.
- *Vary use of paired distractors.* Methods of constructing distractors should be varied throughout the test so that patterns do not emerge to assist the student. For example, pairing the key (B) with its opposite (A) (box 3.8) is not advisable. If the pattern in box 3.8

BOX 3.6

Minimizing Reading

How long will Joe stay in Bali at his grandfather's house?

Not this	But this
Carl went to	Carl and his family went to the
A the river with his family.	**A** river.
B the beach with his family.	**B** beach.
C the country with his family.	**C** country.
D the mountains with his family.	**D** mountains.

BOX 3.7

Item with a Negative Stem

What did Mario's parents say Mario could **not** have in their house?

A his pet dog

B his smelly shoes

C the horse blanket

D a basket of fruit

BOX 3.8

Poorly Paired Distractors

Tom didn't like the coat because it was

A too big.

B too small.

C the wrong color.

D not warm enough.

BOX 3.9

Dealing with Pairs in Distractors

Tom didn't like the coat because it was too

A big.

B light.

C small.

D heavy.

---

recurs throughout the test, it will become obvious to some test-wise students that they need only consider the paired distractors (A and B). One solution is to write some items in which the key is not one of the paired opposites. Another solution is to include two pairs of opposites in the item, as shown in box 3.9.

- *Avoid using certain distractors.* Distractors that contain words such as *always* and *never, none of the above,* and *all of the above* should be avoided because they are usually easy for students to rule out.

- *Use a suitable number of distractors.* Develop items with a key and four plausible distractors (five options in all), if possible, and then pretest all the distractors. Use the distractors that have the best statistical properties (see volume 4 of this series, *Analyzing Data from a National Assessment of Educational Achievement*).

- *Vary the position of the key.* The position of the key should vary from one item to the next. There should be no obvious pattern in its location. The options may be arranged from shortest to longest or from longest to shortest, or they may be randomly ordered. Ensure that the key is not always the longest option.

Good options have the following characteristics:

- They are of similar length and are written in a similar style to the key. The key must not stand out among the distractors because of its length, wording, or other superficial quality.
- They vary in style from item to item. They are not repetitive.
- They do not give a clue to the answer to another item.
- They do not include partially correct distractors, such as paired options, where each distractor contains one incorrect and one correct option.
- They do not mislead or confuse through lack of clarity or ambiguity.
- They do not overlap in meaning. The distractors must have different meanings from one another. Distractors should not be synonyms. A particular meaning in one distractor should not be included in the general meaning of another distractor.
- They include a key that is indisputably correct or a defensible accurate response to the question and not simply the best of the options presented.
- They have distractors that are indisputably incorrect, while being reasonable and plausible. Any distractor that is absurdly wrong reduces the number of real choices available to the student and contributes nothing to the item.

Writing Short-Response Items

Short-response items should be clearly focused to elicit the skill they are intended to assess. Good short-response items are clear and precise. Scoring guides should be developed at the same time as the items. The accompanying CD contains examples of scoring guides for short-response items. See, for instance, *PISA Mathematics Released Items 2006* and *Reading International Grade 4 PIRLS 2001 Sample Items Scoring Guide*.

Short-response items are usually classified as open ended when one or two sentences or several additions to a diagram are required for a correct answer. Open-ended items usually have a range of possible correct answers. Short-response items are classified as closed response when one or two words or a line on a diagram are sufficient for the answer. Closed-response items usually have a very limited set of correct answers.

Open-ended items should address substantial skills in key curriculum areas to justify the test time that students will need to respond to them. Students should still be able to give brief correct responses to open-ended items. Most of the time students spend on an item should be devoted to working out a solution rather than to recording their response.

Considering what a wrong answer might be is important in a short-response item. If all conceivable coherent answers are likely to be correct, the item may do little to contribute to the assessment of a particular skill. The item should be constructed to ensure that there are plausible incorrect answers.

Ensure that short-response items have more than two possible responses. Items for which only two possible options exist, such as "open" or "shut," give students a 50 percent chance of guessing the correct answer. Such an item could be extended by asking students to give reasons for their answers. The item could then be scored on the basis of the correct selection of "open" or "shut" *and* the explanation. Students who select the correct option but who do not give an explanation would receive a zero score.

Items should not provide extensive assistance to the reader in understanding the meaning of the stimulus. For example, an item should not summarize the key ideas in a paragraph of the stimulus or make an inference in the stimulus explicit. Quoting from the stimulus is preferable, rather than summarizing or interpreting meaning.

A danger with open-ended items is that students will answer them superficially. The response "because it is important," for instance, could be a technically correct but weak answer to several questions. Sometimes a potentially superficial answer can be included in the question to eliminate it from the range of possible correct responses. For example, an item can be worded as follows: "Why is Jemima's accident important in this story?" Students cannot answer this item "because the accident is important." Instructions, such as "explain your answer" or "give reasons for your answer," are usually necessary for open-ended items to avoid a succinct answer of "yes" or "no."

An effective short-response item should set a clear, specific task that seeks a specific response. The item should allow students to demonstrate their mastery of the requisite skill reasonably quickly. The example in box 3.10 fails to achieve either of these objectives. Students are not told they need to make a box with the largest possible dimensions. This answer, however, is the criterion for a 3-point score. The item is also of poor quality because it is too time consuming. The skills being assessed do not warrant the amount of time that students would need to experiment with possibilities and arrive at the correct answer. The problem needs to be simplified so that students can demonstrate the relevant skills efficiently.

When a student does not respond to a particular item for one of a number of reasons (such as skipping it because it was considered

---

BOX 3.10

Confusing Open-Ended Item with Unclear Directions

An open box is to be made from a rectangular hard paper, 150 cm by 100 cm, by cutting out equal-size squares on each corner and using masking tape to connect the edges. What size square will you cut from the corner? Provide reason(s) for choosing this size

_____

_____

Scoring guide: The number of points ranges from 0 to 3.

3 points: describes a square of side 20 cm and a box with dimensions 110 cm by 60 cm by 20 cm; also explains that *this size of box has the largest capacity*

2 points: describes a 20-cm square to be cut on every corner but offers no explanation

1 point: describes any possible size of square with one side less than 50 cm

0 points: gives dimensions for a square that are greater than 50 cm (an impossible response)

9 missing

difficult or not having an opportunity to attempt it because the item was not in the assigned test booklet), a code value (not a score) of 9 is often assigned to denote missing data. Missing data are covered in some detail in volume 3, *Implementing a National Assessment of Educational Achievement.*

Short-response items should be clearly and simply worded (see box 3.11).

Developing Scoring Guides for Partial-Credit Items

Responses to some short-response questions have two or more categories of correct response. These are known as partial-credit items. The scoring guide should differentiate between more comprehensive, precise, or sophisticated responses and incomplete or partially correct responses. The better answers are given a higher score. The example in box 3.12 is the scoring guide for a partial-credit item for drawing a square that can be scored up to 3 points.

The following types of items may be scored as partial credit:

- Students are asked to give two reasons for a character's behavior. Students who give two correct reasons are given a score of 2, and students who give one correct reason receive a score of 1.
- Students are given a higher score for a more sophisticated understanding; for example, a 2-point score in a reading test could reflect understanding of the irony in a piece of text, whereas a 1-point score is given for a literal reading of the text.

BOX 3.11

Good Example of a Closed Constructed-Response Item

Each person digs at the same rate.

One person can finish digging a garden in 12 hours.

Two people can finish digging the same garden in 6 hours.

How long does it take 4 people? _____

How long does it take x people? _____

BOX 3.12

Item with Partial Credit

The length of the side of a square is 10 cm.

Draw this square in the space below. Use your ruler.

Scoring guide:

3 points: draws a square with 4 sides 10 cm length and 4 right angles

2 points: draws a rectangle with 2 sides 10 cm length and 4 right angles

1 point: draws a 4-sided shape with 2 sides 10 cm length but no right angles

0 points: draws any other shape

9 missing

- A 2-point score may include identification of both the cause and the consequence, whereas a 1-point score requires correct identification of only one of these.
- In mathematics, a score of 3 is given for the correct solution to a problem and an appropriate explanation of the method, a score of 2 is given for the correct solution without an explanation, and a score of 1 is given for a description of an appropriate method with incorrect calculations.

The distinction between full- or partial-credit scores should be clear. Ensure that examples of 1-point answers, given in the scoring guide, are not simply poorly worded or brief responses that actually satisfy the 2- or 3-point criteria. Clarifying the difference between 1-point answers and incorrect answers is also important. This distinction can be the most difficult to make in scoring some partial-credit items.

The following examples show that open-ended short-response items do not always allow partial credit. The item in box 3.13 shows that while students can give a variety of responses, they can score either 1 or 0 points.

It is important to pretest partial credit items to ensure that the partial credit categories are statistically robust (see chapter 5). An

---

BOX 3.13

Example of an Open-Ended Response Item with Scoring Guide

John and Michael find a tree with 400 mangoes.

John says that Michael now has a 160% chance of hitting a mango.

Do you agree or disagree with John?

Explain.

_____

_____

Scoring guide:

1 point: *Disagrees AND refers to limit of percentage*

Disagree because you cannot get 160%.

Disagree because it's impossible.

Disagree because 100% is the most you can get.

0 points: *Agrees (with or without explanation)*

Disagrees AND doesn't refer to limit of percentage

Disagree because there are more than 160 mangoes.

9 missing

Source: Philippine Department of Education 2004.

---

example of a short-response item with a collapsed scoring guide is presented in box 3.14. In pretesting, a score of 2 points was given for responses of "80%" or "80 percent" and a score of 1 point for students who simply wrote "80." The statistics showed that students who gave the "2-point" answer had a much higher average score on the mathematics test and the students who gave the "1-point" answer had a similar overall average score to those who scored zero on this item. As a result of this pretest information, the scoring guide was changed, and 1 point was awarded to students who responded with "80%" or "80 percent," and zero points to students who responded with 80 or gave another unacceptable response.

BOX 3.14

Example of a Closed-Constructed Item with Scoring Guide

Mango Tree

Michael is trying to hit some mangoes on his farm with his slingshot.

When the tree has 50 mangoes, he has a 20% chance of hitting one.

His chance of hitting a mango doubles when the number of mangoes doubles.

Estimate Michael's chance of hitting a mango in a tree with 200 mangoes.

_____

Scoring guide:

1 point: 80% or 80 percent

0 points: any other answer, including 80 with "%" or "percent" not specified

9 missing

Source: Philippine Department of Education 2004.

Writing Items for Units

Units are groups of items with a common stimulus. A unit might consist of a short story or a graph followed by a set of questions. The basic principles for writing multiple-choice or short-response items apply to items associated with units.

A number of points should be kept in mind when drafting items based on units:

- Items should be independent of each other. Students should not have to answer one item correctly to answer other items correctly.
- Items should not overlap. Each item should assess a clearly different aspect of the stimulus.
- Items should assess a range of skills. For example, items should not repeatedly assess the retrieval of directly stated information or the main idea in each paragraph of the stimulus.
- Items in a unit should cover a range of difficulty levels, starting usually with an easy item.
- Information given in the stem or multiple-choice options of one item should not help the student answer another item.

- Items should assess substantial aspects (and avoid trivial aspects) of the stimulus.
- Items should be on the same page as the unit or on a facing page (in the case of a lengthy stimulus).

Units with eight or more associated items tend to have some duplicate, overlapping, or trivial items. Some items can be deleted during item paneling. Alternatively, the test development team might develop two forms for the pretest by using half the items in one form and the remainder in the second form.

The language section of the accompanying CD contains many examples of units followed by a set of questions. (See, for instance, CD items following "Hare Heralds the Earthquake" from *Reading International Grade 4 PIRLS 2001 Sample Items* or "Petra's Deal" from *Reading Australia Year 3 Sample Questions*.)

PRACTICE ITEMS

Practice items are essential to ensure that students are not penalized because they lack familiarity with the format of items or with the way they should show their answers to the test questions. Usually, the test administrator goes through the practice items with the students, in accordance with very specific instructions in the test administration manual.

When tests include short-response items, it is particularly important that students understand what kind of answers they are expected to give. Students need to understand, for example, where to write their answer to complete a number sequence or how much they are expected to write in response to an item that requires an explanation. Students should be told that they will not be penalized for making minor spelling or grammatical errors, unless that is part of what is being measured. The instructions should encourage them to attempt to answer all items.

Practice questions should be developed for all the response formats in the test. For that reason, practice questions are usually written toward the end of the test development phase, when the kinds of questions that will be in the test are known. The practice items should be *very easy*; for example, students might be asked to write the answer to 2 + 2 on the line shown next to the sum:

$$2 + 2 = \underline{\hspace{2cm}}$$

The emphasis is on how students show their answers. In this case, students must write their answer on the line.

The item panel should review all practice items, which must also be pretested. If several pretest forms are used, the same practice items should be used with each form.

ITEM LAYOUT AND DESIGN

Item layout and design are crucial to the clarity and appeal of a test. Students are more likely to attempt the items in a test that is well presented and easy to read. Test designers should adopt a consistent, pleasing style for layout. A design and layout professional may be employed to create all the images. The accompanying CD provides many examples of well-presented items supported by good-quality artwork.

Basic Guidelines

Following are some basic guidelines for successful test layout and design.

- Use a large font (for example, 36 point) to number the items, so students can easily locate each item.
- Leave adequate space if students need to write an answer. (This is especially necessary for primary school students, who may have large handwriting.)
- Leave sufficient space between items so that students can clearly see where one item ends and the next one begins.
- Use the length of line for an item's answer to indicate how much the students are expected to write. A short line is adequate for a one-word response. Two or three longer lines suggest that the student should provide one or two sentences in response to the item.

- Give each item a unique label, and print this label next to the item number in a small grayscale font in the left margin. A unique identifying label will help ensure accurate tracking of items. Item numbers can change, especially if items appear in multiple test booklets.
- Be consistent in use of single or double quotation marks, italics, underlining, and bold and capital letters.
- Ensure that the layout and images used in pretest items are as close as possible to presentation of items in the final form of the test. Changes in the design and layout of items can affect the difficulty of an item.

Quality of Images

Test images need to be clear, with simple, appropriate language and headings. Images should be drawn by a graphic artist. Scanned images or ones from the Internet are usually not of sufficient quality. Photographs are also generally unsuitable because they add to printing costs. Generally, a graphic artist should redraw photographs. Using the same graphic artist to draw all the images, photographic or otherwise, gives consistency to the layout and design.

Where possible, images should be used to improve clarity and reduce the number of words in an item (see box 3.15). Simple images are most effective. The image should present the concept clearly and cleanly (see box 3.16). It does not have to look lifelike. Line drawings should be used if possible, and extensive shading should be avoided.

Graphs and maps should be labeled clearly and consistently (see boxes 3.17 and 3.18).

As shown in box 3.19, leaving space in graphics allows the stimulus material to be easily read.

In deciding font size and line length, test designers should consider the following:

- Use 14-point type for grades 3 and 4 and 12-point type for higher grades.
- Reduce the width of stimulus texts to approximately 10 to 14 words per line.
- Ensure line breaks occur in sensible places. Do not allow a single word to fall onto a new line by itself.

BOX 3.15

Using Pictures to Reduce Words

The following image describes a scientific experiment far better than a wordy paragraph might:

Which part of the plant takes in the MOST water?

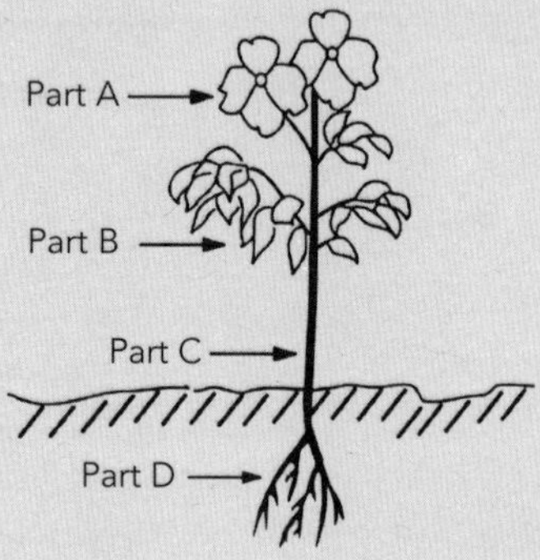

   Ⓐ Part A
   Ⓑ Part B
   Ⓒ Part C
   Ⓓ Part D

S011026

Source: IEA 2007, sample item.

Layout of multiple-choice options should be consistent. Each option should be identified. The following layout options are recommended:

- A vertical column of options labeled from top to bottom:

A

B

C

D

- A horizontal line of options labeled from left to right:
  A   B   C   D

BOX 3.16

Keeping Images Simple

This image conveys a complex system in a simple manner:

Source: Philippine Department of Education 2004.

BOX 3.17

Labeling Graphs Clearly

Clear and consistent labels like those in the following graphic help students comprehend complex questions quickly:

This table shows temperatures at various times on four days.

On which day and at what time was the temperature shown in the table the same as that shown on the thermometer?

TEMPERATURE					
	6 a.m.	9 a.m.	Noon	3 p.m.	6 p.m.
Monday	15°	17°	24°	21°	16°
Tuesday	20°	16°	15°	10°	9°
Wednesday	8°	14°	16°	19°	15°
Thursday	8°	11°	19°	26°	20°

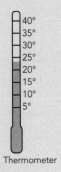

Thermometer

A. Monday, Noon

B. Tuesday, 6 a.m.

C. Wednesday, 3 p.m.

D. Thursday, 3 p.m.

Source: Mullis and others 2000.

BOX 3.18

Labeling Maps Clearly

Care should be taken to label map elements clearly. In the following map, names of continents are shown in all capital letters, while oceans are shown in capital and lowercase letters:

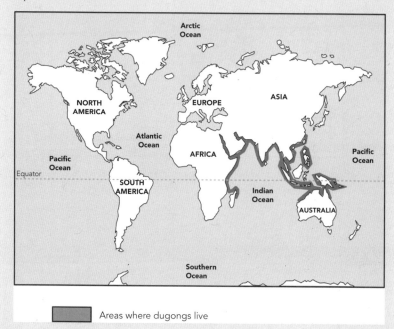

Areas where dugongs live

Source: Papua New Guinea Department of Education 2004.

- Two vertical columns of options, labeled from top to bottom of the first column and then top to bottom of the second column:

A   C

B   D

BOX 3.19

Leaving Space in the Stimulus Material

The space in this drawing lends readability to the stimulus material:

The figure above shows a box that contains a material that could be a solid, a liquid, or a gas. The material is then put into a box four times as large.

Look at the figures below. They show how the different types of material will look when put into the larger box.

A. Identify which figure shows a solid, which shows a liquid, and which shows a gas. (Write the word *Solid*, *Liquid*, or *Gas* on the line next to each figure below. Use each word only once.)

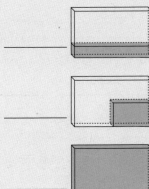

B. Explain your answers.

S031372

Source: IEA 2003, sample item.

THE ITEM-WRITING TEAM

The test development manager leads and manages the item-writing team and supervises the entire program from development and paneling, to pretesting and selection of final test forms. He or she should have good "people" skills and organizational abilities.

The responsibilities of the test development manager include the following:

- Selecting a team of item writers
- Ensuring that the blueprint is understood by the item writers
- Refining the blueprint
- Establishing a set of rules or protocols for presenting, classifying, and storing items
- Ensuring that item writers are aware of the amount of page space items can occupy
- Establishing and monitoring the item panel processes
- Monitoring item development progress against the test blueprint
- Reviewing items with expert groups or key stakeholders
- Monitoring the quality of items
- Tracking item development against timelines
- Recording details of all items developed, including pretest history and changes made during analysis
- Ensuring that the blueprint is reflected in the final test.

Item writing requires attention to detail, creativity, intellectual rigor, depth of content knowledge, and good understanding of students' development in a learning area. Ideally, item writers should demonstrate the following traits:

- They should show initiative and willingness to conduct an extensive search for interesting stimulus materials, and they should be able to develop high-quality stimulus materials.
- They should have a capacity to accept feedback on their work and to comment on the work of other item writers with the same degree of critical detachment.
- They should demonstrate a desire for excellence and a willingness to attend to details when developing and refining items.

An initial screening test is worth considering when selecting item writers. The test might consist of giving potential writers 30 minutes to generate items that are based on a set of stimulus materials. This test may be followed by an interview during which candidates are asked to explain the reasoning behind their responses to the screening test. The interview panel might check the readiness of prospective item writers to accept criticism of their work.

Ideally, some experienced item writers should be involved in the training of new item writers. These experienced writers may have to be recruited from another country as consultants if no one with appropriate expertise is available within the country. Consultant item writers might run training sessions, review items as they are developed, or do both. Item writers working full time after training can take several months to reach the point where they begin to produce items of reasonable quality.

The following questions should be addressed in training:

- What is the overall purpose of the test?
- What are appropriate stimulus contexts for the items?
- Which strands of the curriculum will the test address?
- What proportion of items will address different aspects of the curriculum?
- What language (or languages) will be used?
- What is an appropriate level of simplicity in the vocabulary and grammar used?
- Which item formats will be used, and in what proportions?
- What are the publication specifications (number of pages in the test booklet, page size, number of items per page)?
- How many items are proposed for the final version of the test?
- How many items have to be developed?
- How will the draft test items be reviewed?
- What is the time frame for development, pretesting, and selection of final forms?
- Should any culturally sensitive issues or constraints be considered in drafting stimulus material and items?

Item writers should have a shared understanding of the answers to these questions. They should also consistently monitor their own and others' work. All item writers should have copies of the finalized test blueprint as well as a common understanding of its contents.

Specifying the style of item presentation in detail from the outset saves much time in the long run. The test development manager should set up a style sheet that specifies exactly how items and scoring guides are to be presented. The style sheet should cover all aspects of layout, including the selection of fonts, the size of fonts, the use of indentations, the placement of headings, and the kinds of details that must be included, as shown in the example in box 3.20.

This guide shows that item writers need to give their unit a heading using Arial bold 16 point with capital letters. The rest of the text for the item is in Times New Roman. Most of it is 12 point. The question

---

BOX 3.20

Example of Style Sheet for Item Writers

EASTER TRADITIONS (heading, 16 point Arial bold)

Question 1: Easter Traditions (subheading, 12 point Times New Roman bold)

What did people give each other on Easter Sunday? (question, 12 point Times New Roman bold)

<insert half line> (instruction for publication in italics and parentheses)

Text Type	Item Format	Process
Information	Closed constructed	Retrieval

(table with 3 columns and 2 rows: column headings, 12 point Times New Roman bold, body of table, 12 point Times New Roman no bold)

Scoring Guide (subheading, 12 point Times New Roman bold)

1 point: *refers to eggs* (12 point Times New Roman italics)

- They gave each other eggs. (bullet, 10 point Times New Roman)

- They decorated eggs.

0 points: *refers to pancakes, other, or vague*

- pancakes.

- They gave each other things.

should be labeled, in bold, "Question 1." The unit name should follow as shown. The item and space for the student response are under the question. The item writer inserts and completes a table to show the text type, item format, and process students use to answer the item. The scoring guide is labeled as shown. The criteria for the score points are given in italics with examples of student responses given as indented bullet points in 10 point. By following the guide, item writers can help ensure that pretest and final items are prepared in a consistent, streamlined, and efficient manner.

Item writers need regular, clear feedback and constructive direction about their own items and the way they match the blueprint so that they can learn from their mistakes, develop their skills, and refine their items. Item writers must meet regularly and often in item panels to critique their work. The test manager must be prepared to replace writers who are not able to develop high-quality items after a reasonable training period.

ITEM PANELS

An item panel consists of a small group (between three and six) of item writers who jointly review material that one or more of them have developed. The panel's objective is to accept, modify, or reject the material. The team approach, which is part of the quality control process, helps get multiple perspectives on individual items. Unless item writers are highly experienced, items usually undergo substantial revision after a panel review.

Panel members should prepare their critiques before the item panel meets. They should have ample time to examine items and draft suggested improvements.

The panel should carefully critique the context of the stimulus material, content, wording, language, layout, and illustrations to ensure that every aspect of the stimulus is relevant to the blueprint, is worthy of inclusion in the test, and is clear and concise. Then, they should thoroughly examine every item to ensure that the wording is unambiguous and the format appropriate and that the item clearly addresses skills and content areas specified in the blueprint. The set of items is also examined to consider how well the overall balance of items reflects the blueprint. Panel members should explore every possibility of improving the stimulus and the items and, where necessary, make suggestions for new items.

During the item-panel process, item writers should explain their work and should be prepared to accept constructive criticism. The panel leader should ensure that broad agreement exists about changes to be made in individual items. Item writers should document the suggested changes and subsequently revise the items.

A language expert may be needed on panels where item writers are writing tests that are not in their first language. The language expert needs a good understanding of the language skills of the target test population.

A subject expert may be included in a panel, especially if the content area is complex. Involving a subject expert in some panels may be useful to clarify content issues, but this involvement may not need to be continuous. The subject expert is unlikely to be concerned with the finer points of item writing.

It is advisable not to include policy makers and key stakeholders in item panels. The finer details of panel deliberations are not their concern.

Panel members should consider every aspect of an item:

- Is the right content being assessed?
- Is the item format appropriate for the targeted students?
- Is the item substantive, or is it trivial?
- Is the item wording clear and unambiguous?
- Are there spelling errors or omitted words?
- If the item is multiple choice, are the options similar and meaningful?
- If the item is multiple choice, is the correct answer clearly and unambiguously obtained from the given information (the stem, the stimulus material, or both)?
- Is the item layout attractive and uncluttered?
- Do most of the items have a difficulty that will allow approximately 40 to 80 percent of the tested students to give the correct answer?
- If the item requires partial-credit scoring, is each score likely to attract at least 10 percent of the respondents?

- Does the item seem to be unbiased and fair for major subgroups in the targeted population?

The panel should also consider ways to improve the item:

- Shorten it.
- Add more information.
- Change expression or wording.
- Add a diagram or picture.
- Recast it in a different item format.

Item writers should receive regular and frequent feedback from the time they begin developing items. Item panels should meet once a week if possible.

Revising materials can be a complex task. The panel needs a leader to ensure that recommendations are unanimous and that a consensus is reached on changes to be made. The item writer is not the correct person to decide which changes are adopted or disregarded. The panel leader's recommendations should be sufficiently precise to ensure that the item writer is clear about what changes to make.

Reworking other people's items can become heated at times. The panel leader should focus discussion on item improvement and ensure that the panel works constructively toward this objective.

All panel members, including experienced item writers, should have their work reviewed. It is normal, especially for new item writers, to expect suggestions for extensive revisions. Critiquing items should not be seen as a criticism of an individual. Item writers who cannot engage in robust discussion and reworking of their items should be replaced.

OTHER REVIEWERS

Expert groups or key stakeholders should have the opportunity to review the pool of items several times during item development. This procedure can help ensure that the test items are of good quality and are consistent with the blueprint. The test development manager usually presents all the items, or a selection, to a reference group selected for this purpose.

The first review with the reference group should take place reasonably early in the item development process to ensure that item writers are working in the right direction. The reference group may suggest refinements to some aspects of the blueprint, especially if item writers are having difficulties meeting some of the specifications. Item writers may also need more specific direction about acceptable and unacceptable material.

A review is normally conducted after all the items have been drafted to ensure that key stakeholders approve the items before the pretesting takes place. A final review allows key stakeholders to approve the selection of items for the final test form.

TRACKING ITEMS

Keeping track of items is critical. Each item should have a unique label so that it can be tracked through each stage from pretesting to analysis.

Approximately two and one-half to three times more items need to be developed than are required for the final test forms. It is usually necessary to produce multiple booklets at each grade level for the pretest. Some of the same items must appear in different booklets. This allows all the pretest items to be linked onto the same scale and compared. The label of each item must be independent of the order of the item in the booklet so that items duplicated in different booklets and unique items can be identified clearly.

Tracking items through the analysis stage can be complicated. If the analyst fails to give a unique label to an item, the item can be very difficult to trace. Computer software can compound the problem. The software usually numbers items automatically. If items are dropped from the pretest analysis, the software will renumber the items so that the number of an item in the analysis may no longer correspond to the number in the initial analysis or to the number in the test booklet. Giving each item the same unique label in the test booklet and in each of the analyses will help prevent this problem.

Item labels should be as meaningful as possible. The test development manager should coordinate with the data analyst to establish how many characters can be used for a label. Software analysis packages have different limits. The following labeling convention is used by one testing agency for a test of reading, writing, and mathematics administered over several years:

- The first character is R, M, or W for Reading, Mathematics, or Writing.
- Characters 2 and 3 indicate the year the item was administered (for example, 07 for 2007).
- Characters 4, 5, and 6 signify the item (starting with 001).

For example, M06003 indicates that the item is a mathematics test item administered in 2006 and it is the third item in the item pool.

Items should be labeled during development. The same label should be printed in the pretest booklets and final forms. Labels can be printed in a small font in grayscale in the margin opposite the item numbers in test booklets, as shown below:

M06003   **5**   Complete this sum.

6 + 7 = _____

It is essential to keep a complete history of each item that is developed. The data analyst needs a record of the keys for multiple-choice items and the location of items in pretest booklets. Reports often require information about the format of items and the processes that each item assessed. The test development manager should set up and maintain a spreadsheet to keep a record of each item, its classifications and status, and any changes that may have been made to the item.

The following is an example of some of the column headings in a spreadsheet record of all reading items for a test:

- **unit name**   name given to unit (for example, "Racing Cars")
- **item label**   6-digit label (for example, R06003)
- **item content**   wording of the test question
- **current status**   description indicating whether the item is available for use (for example, released as a practice item, rejected by client, copyright permission refused)
- **key**   correct answer for a multiple-choice question
- **max score**   maximum score points for the item

- **text type**   text genre (for example, narrative, information)
- **item format**   format of the test question (for example, multiple choice)
- **process**   cognitive process (for example, retrieving)
- **analysis notes**   changes made to the item after pretest

Items should be stored in a secure location. All relevant material associated with the development of a unit or an item should be stored with that item. Even material that is not used in the pretest should be kept, because it may be used later at the same or other grade levels. The source of documents or illustrations should be recorded and stored with the unit or item so that copyright permission can be sought if necessary. Copies of original documents should be kept so that any subsequent modifications can be identified.

Most items can be stored electronically. As a precaution, keep backup files of items on a separate computer or disc. Correct labeling and full and accurate classification help ensure that items are stored in the appropriate (computer) file folders and can be easily retrieved by others. Items tend to undergo constant revision, including changes to scoring guides and illustrations as well as minor improvements in wording. The latest version of the item should be readily apparent from the information in the file folder.

NOTES

1. For further information on constructing test items, see Chatterji (2003), Haladyna (1999), Kubiszyn and Borich (2000), and Linn and Miller (2004).
2. The U.S. National Assessment of Educational Progress includes a writing component (National Assessment Governing Board n.d.).

CHAPTER 4

PRETESTING ITEMS

Test construction for a national assessment uses, for the most part, the technology that has been developed in the design of tests intended to assess and report on the achievements of individual students. Since such tests are used to discriminate between the performances of students, all students will take essentially the same test. The purpose of a national assessment is quite different: to describe the extent to which students in an education system as a whole (or a clearly defined part of it) have acquired the knowledge and skills prescribed in a curriculum, not to discriminate among students. To do this, the test should provide adequate curriculum coverage, which may require a much larger sample of the curriculum than is required in tests designed to assess individual students. The need for extensive curriculum coverage is reinforced when an assessment sets out to identify areas of the curriculum in which students exhibit strengths and weaknesses.

To address these issues, many national and international assessments use a much larger number of items than one finds in a test designed to assess individual students. However, to avoid placing too great a burden on individual students, each student responds to only a fraction of the total number of items in the assessment. Hence, several alternative sets of items in a rotated booklet design have to be provided. The precise number varies from one national assessment to another.

This approach, though desirable in many ways, carries with it a number of complications for the administration of a national assessment. First, test design is complex, because item overlap and matches between subsamples have to be ensured. Second, administration is more complex because it is necessary to ensure that booklets are given to the right students and that the instructions given to students are appropriate for all booklets. Finally, combining data from multiple sets of items requires relatively complex statistical procedures. For those reasons, many developing countries have not used multiple test booklets in their national assessments.

Most of the comments in the following pages and also in chapter 5 apply both to situations in which a national assessment team uses multiple test booklets and to those in which it opts for a single test booklet to measure learning achievement in a subject area. Both approaches require great attention to careful pretesting.

Pretesting or pilot-testing is an essential element of test development. A pretest is administered to students with the same characteristics as those who will be taking the final test. Schools of different sizes, in different areas, with students from varying socioeconomic backgrounds should be included. Ideally, the pretest is conducted a year in advance, at the same time of year as the scheduled final test. For example, the pretest might be given to grade 5 students in October 2005 and the final test to grade 5 students in October 2006. In practice, this scenario may not be possible, and the pretest may be conducted with students who have a few months more or less school experience than the target population. For example, grade 6 students may be pretested early in the school year to provide data for a test that will be administered to grade 5 students at the end of the school year.

Students who participate in the pretest should not take the final test. If the final test is to be administered to a statistically selected random sample, the final sample should be drawn before selecting schools for the pretest.

It is good practice to pretest two or three times the number of items required for the final test. The length of each of the pretest forms should be similar to those of the final test. Labeling forms alphabetically according to the grade level is helpful; for example, five grade 3 forms would be labeled as forms 3A, 3B, 3C, 3D, and 3E, and five grade 8 forms as 8A, 8B, 8C, 8D, and 8E.

Several pretest forms will be required at each grade level. Ideally, the forms for each grade level should be randomly distributed in each class. If three grade 5 forms (5A, 5B, and 5C) are used, each school should receive a mix of all three forms. If this procedure is not possible, ensuring that each form is distributed across the whole cross-section of the pretest sample is important. For example, form 5A should not be given to city students only, form 5B to rural students in the north, and form 5C to rural students in the south. Forms should be as equivalent as possible in terms of the test blueprint.

Linking the pretest forms is essential so that the items can be pooled for comparison. Linking means that some of the same items appear in different forms. Some pretest forms will inevitably be harder than others. By linking forms, the overall difficulty of items can be determined regardless of the form in which they appeared. Horizontal linking is required if testing only one grade level. Vertical linking will be required if more than one grade level is being tested.

A minimum of 200 students should attempt every pretest item at each grade level. If three pretest forms exist for grade 5, then at least 600 students will take the pretest. From the 200 students for every pretest item, at least 150 responses are required. Inevitably, some loss of data will occur during a pretest. For the best of reasons, a school may withdraw from the pretest program at the last minute or administer the test to fewer students than anticipated. It is also unlikely that every student will attempt every item in the pretest.

Because pretesting should be conducted under the same conditions as the final test, the length of time allowed for students to take the test should be the same as will be allowed in the final test. The number of items students can complete in the time allowed may not be known. If so, then assemble a sample pretest form and try it out in a few classes before the pretest is put together to ensure that the number of items in each pretest form is realistic. A national assessment is not a speed test. Most students should have the time to attempt most items.

Try to complete all pretesting over a two- to three-week period.

Pretesting provides the opportunity to assess the appropriateness and quality of items. It also allows many aspects of test administration to be fine-tuned. Pretest administrators should be asked to provide the following information:

- Did students have sufficient practice questions, and were the instructions and explanations sufficiently clear?
- Was the test the right length or too long, and approximately how many students finished more than 10 minutes early?
- Did students appear to be engaged by the test?
- Did students have sufficient resources, such as pencils or erasers?
- Were school facilities suitable for conducting a test?
- Did teachers and students understand the purpose of the test?

DESIGNING THE PRETEST FORM

The analysis of the pretest data provides the basis for selecting items for the final test. Many national assessments prepare different forms of linked test booklets for each grade level. This approach helps give greater curriculum coverage than a single test and, at the same time, helps ensure that students are not subjected to unreasonably lengthy tests. Test design and linking must be done properly to ensure that data can be combined onto a single scale. The data analyst, statistician, or main computer professional needs to be involved in the design of the pretest to help ensure that data requirements are met.[1]

Linked forms share common items. Between 8 and 10 common items are normally required. There are several ways of linking forms.

With a *single common set of link items*, the same 8 to 10 link items are repeated in each form. Note that if the link items behave poorly (have poor statistical characteristics) in the analysis, the linking of the forms will be weak, and the quality of the overall analysis will consequently be undermined.

A second way is *circular linking*. Different sets of items are used between pairs of forms. For example, form 3A may be linked to form 3B with set *X* of items, form 3B to form 3C with set *Y* of items, and form 3C back to form 3A with set *Z* of items. Each form also

FIGURE 4.1

Example of Circular Linking of Items

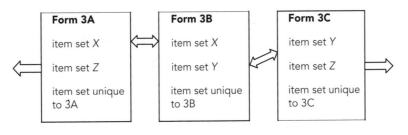

Source: Authors' representation.

contains unique items that do not appear in either of the other forms (figure 4.1).

A third way is *linear linking*, which follows the circular linking model but excludes the set Z item links. Thus, form 3A would be linked to 3B, and 3B linked to 3C, but no link would occur between forms 3A and 3C.

If it is unclear how the items will perform, use of circular linking and more link items than necessary is preferable. In circular linking, even if one set of link items fails, links between the forms will be preserved.

Linking can be both horizontal (at one grade level) and vertical (at different grade levels—for example, between grades 3 and 5). If the final forms are not going to be vertically linked, then pretest linking should emphasize strong horizontal links. Minimal vertical linking may be included to allow comparison of pretest data between grade levels. Technically, only 8 or 10 items in common are necessary between the grade levels. Estimating what makes a good vertical link item is more difficult than estimating what makes a good horizontal link. Because this is a pretest and the quality of the link items is unknown, having at least 16 vertical link items, spread across each of the forms, is advisable.

If the final forms are to be vertically linked, having many more vertical link items in the trial than will be required in the final test is important, so that the best link items can be selected for the final form. An alternative pretest model for vertically linked final forms is shown in figure 4.2. The model is based on randomly distributing forms A, B, and C within each class.

FIGURE 4.2

Model for Vertically Linking Items

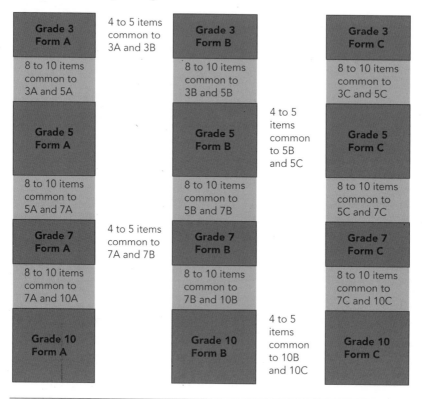

Source: Authors' representation.

In this rather elaborate example, forms 3A, 5A, 7A, and 10A are each vertically linked in linear fashion with 8 to 10 items. Items are linked in a similar fashion in forms B and C. There are altogether 8 to 10 horizontal link items between the A and B forms at grade 3 and grade 7 and altogether 8 to 10 horizontal link items between the B and C forms at grade 5 and grade 10. This number of horizontal links is acceptable. If the test forms are not going to be randomly distributed within each class, or if the item writers are unsure of the quality of the horizontal link items, more horizontal links should be included at each grade level.

Link items should be placed toward the beginning or the middle of test forms rather than at the end to prevent a situation in which students may not respond to the items. Link items should be placed in a similar order in each of the booklets and in a similar position in the test booklets so that any differences in student performance cannot be attributed to the order or position of the items. Small differences in the location of link items are inevitable. Large differences should be avoided.

Link items should be in the average difficulty range. In general, students of average ability in the target population should have between 40 and 60 percent likelihood of answering these items correctly. Because this is a pretest, the difficulty of the items for the pretest population will not be known; item writers will have to make their best estimate of item difficulty. If item writers are uncertain about the accuracy of their estimates, increasing the number of link items is advisable.

If the items are arranged in units, it is best to link forms with items taken from two or more units, in case items associated with one unit do not work well. It is not necessary to use all the items from a unit for linking; some items may be common and others unique, as shown in table 4.1. Both units "Finding a Pet" and "Mount Avarapa" appear in grade 3 forms 3A and 3B. Three items are common to each unit and each form. The pretest has additional unique items.

If the pretest includes a mix of item formats, the link items should also reflect this mix.

Items should have unique labels printed in grayscale next to the item in each test form in which the item appears. Items with the same label should be identical in every respect except for their order of appearance in a test form. Items with slight variations in their wording should have different labels.

The item writer should create a spreadsheet with a list of all the items; separate headings should show which items appear in which forms and in what order. Table 4.2 shows part of a sample spreadsheet that covers three units ("Dogs," "Ellie," and "Bang") of a grade 5 reading

TABLE 4.1

Link Items in Two Reading Units

Reading units	Items common to 3A and 3B	Items unique to 3A	Items unique to 3B
"Finding a Pet"	3, 4, 6	2, 7	1, 5
"Mount Avarapa"	1, 2, 5	3	4

Source: Authors' representation.

TABLE 4.2

Part of a Spreadsheet for Tracking Items across Forms

Unit name	Item label	Form 5A	Form 5B	Form 5C	Form 5D
"Dogs"	R070101	1	1	4	4
"Dogs"	R070102	3	3	5	5
"Dogs"	R070103		2		
"Dogs"	R070104	2			
"Ellie"	R070201			1	
"Ellie"	R070202			2	1
"Ellie"	R070203			3	2
"Ellie"	R070204				3
"Bang"	R070301	4			6
"Bang"	R070302	5			7

Source: Authors' representation.

test. The items for three units are shown on the left. The numbers in the columns show the order of appearance of each of these items in each of the pretest forms. The first two items in "Dogs" are common to all four forms.

PRINTING AND PROOFREADING THE PRETEST

Each item being pretested should appear as it will appear in the final form. Likewise, stimulus materials, graphics, and illustrations should be presented as they are intended to appear in the final test. Ideally, the order of appearance of link items should be identical, but, in practice, it may vary slightly.

Stimulus material for reading items should appear either (a) on the same page as the items or (b) on the left-hand page, with the items on the right-hand page to allow students to move easily between the items and the text.

The front page of the pretest booklet need not have all the detail required in the final form. It should request information such as a student's school, grade level, gender, language background, and age. Because pretest data are generally not reported, collecting students' names in the pretest is usually not necessary. Some background details that are needed in the final form may not be required for the pretest. Layout of items should be consistent across all the test forms.

The following checklist may be helpful when preparing or reviewing printing of pretest materials:

- Headings (large and clear)
- Margins—top, bottom, left, and right (consistent)
- Page numbers (consistent)
- Item numbers (large and clear)
- Item labels (applied)
- Lines for students to write answers (clear and appropriate length)
- Item wording (font size 12 or 14 points)
- Number of words per line (10 to 12)
- Stimulus material (clear, preferably in a different font from items)
- Stimulus material and associated items (on same or opposite pages)
- Headers and footers (consistent and useful)
- Spelling check (completed).

Some tests include the scoring options in grayscale. For example, 0 or 1 could be given for an item to be scored incorrect or correct, respectively. The scoring option for items that are not attempted is normally 9, as discussed in chapter 3. Raters can simply circle the appropriate score. Inserted scores remind raters of the range of scoring options.

All test booklets and administration manuals must be thoroughly proofread. Proofreaders should attempt the test items as though they were taking the test. They should ensure that the materials meet the following criteria:

- Initial instructions and practice items are clear and unambiguous.
- Items are clear and unambiguous.
- Stimulus material is clear and easy to read.
- Multiple-choice options include one correct answer with other options all clearly incorrect.
- Each of the multiple-choice options makes sense.
- An appropriate space is provided for students to record answers, if required.
- The stimulus material for reading is on the same page as the items or on a left-hand page with the items on the opposite right-hand page.

- The items in a unit are independent; that is, the answer to one item is not given in the stem or options of another item.
- Link items are identical.
- No spelling or grammatical errors occur.
- The layout of the various test forms is consistent.

Proofreading is critical. Serious errors can and have occurred at virtually all stages of the pretesting process. A pretest represents a serious waste of time, effort, and funds if it contains typographical errors and inconsistencies. It reduces the usefulness of the data, because incorrect pretest items cannot be used in the final form of the test. Therefore, using skilled proofreaders and allowing sufficient time for proofreading and revision are important.

Pretest booklets should be checked when returned from the printer. Random checks should be made of each bundle or box of booklets to ensure the following:

- All pages have been printed clearly.
- Pages appear in the correct order.
- Pages have not been duplicated.
- The reading stimulus for each unit is on the correct page.
- Illustrations are clear.

Pretest booklets should be printed and checked well before they are sent out to schools. This schedule will allow time for reprinting, if necessary. Because pretest print runs are generally small, reprinting, if required, is a relatively small cost item.

IMPLEMENTING THE PRETEST

Students must not have any doubt about how to show their answers to each item or question at the pretest or final test stages. The tests are designed to test knowledge of an important curriculum area—not students' abilities to guess how to show their answers. Students should be given adequate opportunity during pretesting, both at the beginning of the pretest and at the beginning of sections within the pretest, to do practice items. Giving students in education systems that do not have a tradition of multiple-choice-type testing an adequate number (for example, three or four) of practice items is particularly important.

The number of items in the pretest forms can be the same or slightly fewer than in the final forms. It is important that all students attempt all the items in the pretest. If the pretest is too long, or if the pretest has too many hard items toward the end, then few of the items at the end of the test will have responses.

Begin each form with some easy items to encourage weaker students to attempt the test. It is often desirable to mix the difficulty of subsequent items so that students persist rather than abandon the whole test when they come to a series of difficult items. Try to make the overall difficulty of each pretest form roughly similar. Avoid any one form being full of hard items, because students may give up. If that happens, the items at the end of the form will not have sufficient data for pretest analysis purposes.

Pretesting offers the opportunity to test alternative versions of items in different forms. For example, an item may be pretested in a multiple-choice and an open-ended format (box 4.1).

Different wordings of open-ended items may also be pretested. Note that alternative versions of items should not be used as link items; link items must be identical.

SCORING THE PRETEST

The purpose of collecting pretest or pilot data is to obtain information that will help select good-quality items for the final test. Generally,

---

BOX 4.1

Example of an Item in Multiple-Choice and Open-Ended Format

13 + 17 + 8 =

(A) 28   (B) 30   (C) 38   (D) 110

OR

13 + 17 + 8 = _____

scores and students' names need not be linked. The main issues for pretest scoring are quality control and consistency in treatment of students' responses.

All scoring requires quality control procedures. Doing pretest scoring and data entry by hand is usually economical because the number of items is manageable. Raters and data entry personnel should be properly trained. The test development manager should see to it that the quality of their work is checked twice a day to ensure consistency and reliability. Checks may be made more frequently at the early stages and perhaps less frequently at later stages if a rater's work is found to be satisfactory.

Knowing the percentage of students who did not attempt pretest items provides useful information about how to structure the final form of the test. The following are general guidelines relating to this issue:

- If 15 percent or more of students did not attempt several items at the end of a test, the pretest may have been too long. Consider making the final test easier, shorter, or both.

- If 15 percent or more of students did not attempt an item that is not at the end of the test, something may be wrong with the way the item was presented, or it may be too difficult. Possibly, students may have overlooked the item, did not know how to show their answer, or did not understand the wording. Consider revising and pretesting a new item.

- If a certain group in the population (for example, 15 percent or more of girls) did not attempt an item but most others did, the item may be biased. Consider not including it in the final test.

- If 15 percent or more of students consistently did not attempt to answer items in a particular format (for example, open-ended items), these students either may not have understood how to show their answers or may have needed opportunities to learn how to answer this kind of item. Consider adding additional practice or sample items using this format and pretesting these items again.

Generally, missing or no-attempt scores are shown as 9. Ensure no items in the test have a possible correct score of 9. If they do, X (or another alphabet letter) may be used to denote missing scores.

Scorers and raters need to be clear about the rules for scoring missing responses. A missing response is usually one where the student has not made any pencil marks at all. Any attempt to answer an item, even if it is illegible or unintelligible, is usually treated as incorrect rather than missing.

Scoring guides for multiple-choice items should be designed to enable the test developer or reviewer to get as much useful data as possible from each item.

A four-option multiple-choice item, for instance, might be coded 1, 2, 3, 4, 8, or 9. More numbers can be used to reflect more options. The numbers 1, 2, 3, and 4 indicate the option the student selected. A code value of 7 can be used to show that a student selected two or more options and possibly does not understand how to answer a multiple-choice item. In book 4 in this series, *Analyzing Data from a National Assessment of Educational Achievement*, we use a code value of 8 to indicate that the student did not attempt the item and 9 to show that the particular item was not administered to the student (as it was in another test form) and therefore should not be scored as incorrect.

Multiple-choice items should never be entered into a computer as correct or incorrect. The layout of the multiple-choice items should have an implicit numbering pattern from 1 to 4 or 5, depending on the number of options.

The rater or the data entry person simply records the (implicit) number of the option the student selected for each multiple-choice item. The rater or data entry person does not need to know what the

---

BOX 4.2

Example of a Data Entry Sheet for a Pretest

Student	Q1	Q2	Q3	Q4	
					Order of appearance of questions in the test form
Ahmed Buta	2	3	2	1	
Miriam Wisim	4	3	2	4	Options selected by each student for each item
Almet Duras	2	3	1	4	

Source: Authors.

correct option is or whether the student's response is correct or incorrect. A data entry sheet might look like the example in box 4.2.

The item writer must provide the data analyst with a list of the correct options or key for each item, which the data analyst enters into the software program. The analysis software then computes each student's response as correct or incorrect, according to the list of keys.

Knowing which incorrect options students select gives item writers important information about the quality of multiple-choice items and their possible usefulness for the final test form. For example, if almost no students select either of two incorrect options, these two options evidently are not functioning as effective distractors.

Closed constructed-response and open-ended items are usually scored as 0 (incorrect), 1 (correct), or 9 (missing). A partial-credit item might be scored 0, 1, 2, or 9.

Hand-scoring pretest items requires training and quality control similar to hand-scoring the final test. An experienced item writer should conduct the training and oversee the scoring of pretest items. The accompanying compact disc contains examples of scoring guides for language, mathematics, and science open-ended items.

Item writers must use pretest responses to revise and refine their scoring guides and scoring categories before scoring of the pretest begins. Before hand-scoring begins, item writers should take a sample of completed pretest booklets and compare the actual student responses to short-response items with those anticipated in the scoring guides. Item writers should use the samples to include examples of student responses in their scoring guides. Scoring guides should include incorrect as well as correct responses. The partial-credit scoring guide in box 3.12 shows examples of actual students' responses that match each of the categories of the scoring guide, including zero scores.

Item writers should refine or expand their scoring guides to take account of the range of responses that students actually give. Sometimes these revisions can be quite extensive. Students tend to come up with unanticipated but correct answers or unusual but accurate ways of expressing their ideas. Such examples should be added to the scoring guides, if they are reasonably common. If many students give answers that are difficult to classify as correct or incorrect, item writers need to clarify their scoring guides to make these distinctions clear. A panel or the test development manager should review revised scoring guides before pretest booklets are scored.

During hand-scoring, item writers should receive feedback from raters about any further refinements that might need to be made to the scoring guides. If substantial scoring guide revisions have to be made for an item, the item may have to be rescored, according to the revised scoring guide, to ensure consistency.

It is essential to revise scoring guides so that the criteria for scoring and the examples given match the actual range of student responses. If the scoring guides are not revised, some items will be lost because none of the student responses may meet the overly demanding requirements of the guide. The scoring of other items may be unreliable because raters, not knowing how to score responses if they fall outside the scoring guidelines, will all have made their own individual judgments.

Usually, higher scores for partial-credit items denote a more sophisticated or extensive response. A score of 2 suggests a "better" response than a score of 1. Pretest partial-credit data can be used to collect information about categories of student responses that can help refine pretest items or scoring guides. Responses to a partial-credit pretest item may be coded 0, 1, 2, or 3, although these scores may not be hierarchical. In such nonhierarchical scoring systems, a score of 3 is not considered more sophisticated than a score of 2 or 1. Each of the 1, 2, and 3 scores denotes a correct but different kind of answer. For example, there may be three different ways to solve a mathematics problem. The scoring guide may be quite complex to allow for these three possibilities. If all the pretest students choose the same method, the item writer may revise the scoring guide to focus on the more popular method with a brief reference to other possibilities. The scoring guide would be revised for the final test to show a score of 1 for a correct response, regardless of the method used to solve the problem.

The item writers should inform the data analyst when partial-credit items are used to denote categories rather than hierarchies, which will allow the analyst to differentiate among the responses. The analyst can assign a score of 1 to each correct category response. Thus, it is very important that raters understand when they are scoring partial-credit *hierarchical* items and partial-credit *categories*. All partial-credit items in final tests should be treated as hierarchical.

Volume 4 of this series, *Analyzing Data from a National Assessment of Educational Achievement*, has a special section on analysis of pilot or pretest data. It covers both classical test theory (CTT) and item response theory (IRT) approaches to analysis. IRT is frequently used in analyzing test items, in linking test forms, and in developing scales to report the results of a national assessment (Beaton and Johnson 1989). It has a number of advantages when applied to the scaling of assessment data. IRT allows an item to be characterized independently of any sample of individuals who respond to it and allows an individual respondent to be characterized independently of any sample of items administered to the person. IRT is thus particularly useful when multiple sets of items are administered to students in an assessment. However, it also has some disadvantages—in particular, the complexity of the procedure, which requires considerable skill and experience. When the requisite skill and experience are not available in a country, the application of CTT may be regarded as acceptable.

RELIABILITY

Both pretesting and final testing should report evidence on test reliability. A measure of reliability is an indicator of the consistency of test results. Reliability depends on the quality of test items, the test itself, the way the tests were administered, the characteristics of the group of students (such as the effort they make while taking the pretest or national assessment tests), and the quality of scoring of test items. Reliability is covered in volume 4, *Analyzing Data from a National Assessment of Educational Achievement*.

Test reliability indices range from 0 to 1, where 0 represents a test in which students' responses are entirely inconsistent (for example, a test where all students guess randomly on all items), and 1 represents a test that measures a domain with perfect consistency.

The implementing agency should obtain reliability evidence on the extent to which the individual pretest items correlate with each other. This information will provide a measure of the internal consistency of the test items. Note that this approach assumes the selected items measure a single construct or trait, such as mathematics or language ability. Normally, national and international assessment teams tend to omit items that are not relatively homogenous, that is, ones that do not measure a single construct or trait. Homogeneity can be assessed using an approach such as Cronbach's alpha, Kuder-Richardson formulas 20 or 21, or a spilt-half reliability coefficient, all of which are found in SPSS© statistical software.

If the assessment tests include open-ended or free-response items, the implementing agency should establish that the method of scoring is reliable. The agency should ensure that each rater or corrector of open-ended items is trained to judge whether a student's responses are acceptable. Such training will necessitate that raters work with the test development team to document a list of acceptable and unacceptable answers for each open-ended question. Following training, pairs of raters working independently should score each open-ended item from at least 60 randomly selected pretest booklets, and the percentage of exact agreement among scorers for the overall set of items should be calculated. The implementing agency should seek clarification from the test developers where evidence indicates that raters are confused about whether a particular response is acceptable. Care in scoring open-ended pretest items should help ensure that there is little room for disagreement on acceptable and unacceptable responses when scoring the items in the national assessment. The accompanying compact disc contains a number of examples of scoring open-ended items.

CHAPTER 5

SELECTING TEST ITEMS

The selection of pretest items for the final test (covered in some detail in *Analyzing Data from a National Assessment of Educational Achievement*, volume 4 in this series) depends first, and most importantly, on the framework, especially the blueprint. Second, it depends on the measurement properties of the items.

Typically, the following selection criteria are adopted for each item[1]:

- The item matches the blueprint.
- The percentage of students getting the item correct is in the range of 40 to 80 percent.
- The item shows a low missing-response rate.
- The discrimination index (correlation between the item score and the total test score) is greater than 0.2.
- Test reliability is improved by inclusion of the item in the test.
- Item bias is within acceptable limits for major student groups.

The following considerations are specific to multiple-choice items:

- The point biserial for the key is positive and over 0.2.
- All the distractors are plausible (that is, they have been selected by at least 5 percent of students) and have zero or negative point biserials.

TABLE 5.1

Example of Output from Analysis of a Multiple-Choice Item

Criteria	Option			
	A [0]	B [0]	C [0]	D [1]
Count	90	14	21	254
Percent	23.7	3.7	5.5	67.0
Point biserial	−0.26	−0.21	−0.16	0.39
Mean ability	−0.02	−0.48	−0.14	0.54

Source: Authors' representation.

Table 5.1 shows a typical output from the analysis of a multiple-choice item. Statistically, the item works well.

The column heads show the number of categories or options in the item (A, B, C, D). Option D is the key, or correct option, and is shown with a score of 1 in brackets. Options A, B, and C are shown with scores of 0 in brackets. The row labeled "Count" shows the number of students selecting each option; 254 students selected the correct option. The row labeled "Percent" presents percentage data (the count expressed as a percentage of the number of students). Sixty-seven percent of students selected the correct option. This result shows the item is within an acceptable range of difficulty. The item is fairly easy. Only 3.7 percent of students selected option B, suggesting this option is weak or implausible. Rewriting this option to be more plausible could possibly improve the item; the item would need to be pretested again. The next row shows the point biserial for each option. The point biserial for the correct answer is 0.39. Point biserials for the incorrect options are all negative. In multiple-choice items, the point biserial for the key is the same as the discrimination index for the item. The final row shows the mean ability. The mean ability of the students who selected the correct option is considerably higher than the mean ability of the students who selected the incorrect options. This result also shows that the item is working well.

The following considerations are specific to open-ended items:

• If the item is scored dichotomously, the discrimination index (correlation between the item score and the total score) is greater than 0.2.

- If the item awards partial credit, the discrimination is positive and above about 0.3.
- If the item is scored dichotomously, most items should be in the 40 to 80 percent difficulty range.
- If the item awards partial credit, each score category attracts at least 5 percent of responses.
- If the item awards partial credit, the overall percentage of students who get an item correct, calculated by combining responses to different partially correct categories, is in the range of 40 to 80 percent.
- If the item awards partial credit, the mean ability of the students clearly decreases from the highest to the lowest category of responses for partial-credit items.

A typical output from the analysis of an open-ended partial-credit item with good statistics is shown in table 5.2. The column heads show the categories of student responses. Students scored zero if they answered the item incorrectly. A partially correct answer gained a score of 1, and a fully correct answer received a score of 2. Missing responses are shown as 9 and are also scored as zero. The overall discrimination index is 0.47, which is high. Note that for partial-credit items, the discrimination index is not the same as the point biserial for the highest-score category. The count and the percentage correct are shown in the first two rows. Almost half the students who attempted this item answered it incorrectly. More than 5 percent responded to each of the partial-credit categories, which suggests these categories

TABLE 5.2

Example of Output from Analysis of an Open-Ended Partial-Credit Item

Criteria	Category of student response				Discrimination index = 0.47
	0 [0]	1 [1]	2 [2]	9 [0]	
Count	1,466	425	268	809	
Percent	49.4	14.3	9.0	27.3	
Point biserial	0.09	0.11	0.45	−0.48	
Mean ability	−1.66	0.53	0.90	−1.90	

Source: Authors' representation.

are worth keeping. The point biserial increases from zero to a score of 2, showing that the categories are performing as expected. The mean ability of the students awarded category 2 scores is −0.9. Students awarded category 1 scores have a mean ability of −1.53. The difference is greater than 0.5 and supports maintaining the two categories in the scoring guide because they differentiate between students of quite different ability.

The percentage of students who did not attempt this item is quite high at 27.3 percent. This figure needs to be considered in the context of the pattern of missed items in the whole test. In this instance, most of the open-ended items had missing percentages over 20. Students' unfamiliarity with and reluctance to answer these kinds of item caused the problem, rather than a particular problem with this item.

The overall level of difficulty of the final test should be appropriate for its purpose. A final test that is designed to monitor the performance of all students in the target population should have a range of difficulty that matches the ability of the population. Assessments that are designed for different purposes, such as identifying students who meet a predefined benchmark, may include many easy items or many hard items, depending on where the benchmark is set.

Experience to date in developing national assessment pretests suggests that item writers tend to develop items that, on balance, are too difficult. Part of this tendency may stem from item writers' earlier experiences writing questions for public examinations, where questions tend to be pitched at a relatively high difficulty level. Furthermore, many pretest item writers tend to live in urban areas and do not have an appreciation of the low levels of achievement that can be found in remote rural areas.

If many of the pretest items are too difficult and if the pretest does not have enough easy items to match the criteria in the blueprint, a further round of pretesting with a new set of easier items will be required. Likewise, if there are insufficient difficult items, additional pretesting with harder items is called for.

The person who will analyze the final test data should also analyze the pretest data. Any problems with the way item writers provide information about item classifications and keys or the way items have been scored can be resolved during the pretest analysis.

The item-writing team should be involved in interpretation of the pretest data analysis and in decisions about which items to drop in the final test and which items with weak statistics might need to be included. Decisions about the inclusion or exclusion of items should take into account the blueprint and areas of the curriculum that the test must assess.

Usually, only one final form of a test is used at each grade level. It may consist of two or three separate tests, such as a mathematics test, a reading test, and a writing test. These tests may be combined into a single booklet or printed in separate booklets.

Issues that applied to the pretest regarding the need for link items and their selection and placement will also apply to the final test, if there are several forms.

Some items make excellent conceptual sense but have poor statistics. This result can indicate a problem in the way the item was presented. Students may be unfamiliar with the vocabulary or the way they are required to show their answers, or the stimulus material may be confusing. Ideally, items with very poor statistics should be revised and pretested again. However, when items with poor statistics address important criteria in the blueprint and no other items are available, it may be necessary to include them in the final test.

In principle, items should never be altered between the pretest and the final forms because alteration could affect the item statistics in unknown ways. In practice, test agencies tend to make minor alterations to a few items—generally no more than 4 or 5 in a test of 30 items. Minor alterations might include

- Changing one or two words to improve clarity or to reduce the difficulty of vocabulary
- Dropping the weakest option in a five-option multiple-choice item
- Correcting grammatical errors or improving clarity of expression
- Improving layout, such as the position of labels on a diagram or consistency of headings.

NOTE

1. The examples used in this chapter are based on item analyses using the classical test theory approach. Book 4 in this series *Analyzing Data from a National Assessment of Educational Achievement* covers this approach in some detail. It also features another method of item analysis, item-response theory, which uses a different statistical approach and some different terminology.

CHAPTER 6

PRODUCING THE FINAL TEST

DESIGNING THE FINAL TEST

The data analyst or statistician should be involved in designing the final form. He or she should check that the design meets the following requirements:

- The format in which student background information is supplied on the test cover is appropriate for analysis.
- The method of recording item responses is appropriate for analysis.
- The nature and scope of scoring guides are appropriate for analysis.
- Horizontal links to previous years' test data or vertical links that may be required are statistically sound.

The student background information required on the front cover of the test booklets relates to the purpose of the test and the way test data will be reported. Students should be able to complete the requested information easily and accurately. Front cover information usually includes the following:

- Name of the school
- Student's full name
- Student's gender

- Student's age or date of birth
- Student's grade or class
- Student's language background.

In some countries, students may have unique national identification numbers. These numbers should be used where available.

Including an option on the front cover for the test administrator to record whether students missed all or part of the test through absence or illness or whether students with disabilities were given special assistance to help them write their answers is also useful (see box 6.1).

Generally, ensuring that students' identities are correctly recorded and linked to the appropriate data is easier if the tests for all subjects are kept in one booklet. Potential identification problems are avoided if the single test booklet's cover information is accurately and legibly

---

BOX 6.1

Example of a Test Cover Page

EDUCATION MONITORING ASSESSMENT: GRADE IV

Section for the student to complete:

School _____

Province _____

Grade _____

First name _____

Family name _____

I am a boy. ☐   I am a girl. ☐

Age ☐ years and ☐ months

The language I mostly speak at home is English. Yes ☐   No ☐

Section for the test administrator to complete:

This student was absent for the following tests in this booklet:

Reading ☐

Mathematics ☐

This student received special assistance for Reading ☐   Mathematics ☐

Describe the special assistance provided: _____

Source: Papua New Guinea Department of Education 2004.

entered before the first testing session. If a single booklet is used, the test administrator should take considerable care to ensure that test booklets are handed to the appropriate students before each subsequent testing session.

Effective procedures for matching candidates and booklets are called for if multiple test booklets are used. The following risks are associated with using multiple booklets:

- Students may spell their names differently on different booklets.
- Students may use different names on different booklets, such as a shortened form on one booklet and the full name on others, a religious or cultural name on one booklet and a family name on another, or a first name on one booklet and a middle name on another.
- Students may write all or part of their names illegibly on at least one of the booklets.
- Students may fail to enter their names on one or more of their booklets.

The layout format and test administration guidelines should be clear and consistent. To the extent possible, the pretest layout and the final test layout should be the same.

The test should begin with some easy items to encourage weaker students. Items covering a range of difficulty levels should follow, in no particular pattern, so that students do not struggle with a series of hard items and give up. It is also important that some slower students are given a chance to attempt some of the harder items by placing these items reasonably early in the test. The test should end with some harder items, because students of lower ability are less likely to finish the test. Items referring to a common stimulus (for example, a paragraph or map) should be presented together, irrespective of item difficulty-level considerations.

The guidelines for placement of link items are the same for the final form as for the pretest (see chapter 4). Horizontal link items are necessary to link to a previous test if achievement is being compared over time. Vertical links are required to compare achievement between grade levels. The link items should be placed (a) at the beginning or toward the middle of the booklet and (b) in a similar position in each test booklet.

Item labels should be printed in grayscale on the test booklets so that items can be tracked (see chapter 3).

The test development manager should supply the data analyst with a spreadsheet showing where the items appear in each booklet, including link items.

Decisions about how students will record their answers should have been made when the blueprint was designed (see chapter 2). Frequently, students fill in item responses on the test booklets. The layout of the items should allow adequate space for students to record their answers. The layout of the items should also designate a space for raters to record their scores.

In other instances, especially at the more senior grade levels, separate answer or record sheets may be used. These answer sheets should clearly show how to link the item response or option printed on the test booklet with the appropriate position on the answer sheet. If the items in the test paper are organized in units, organizing the layout of the answer sheets in similar units is helpful.

PRINTING AND PROOFREADING

Factors such as the following determine the length of the test booklet:

- Number of subject areas covered
- Breadth of coverage within subject areas
- Item format
- Use of illustrations
- Length of the stimulus materials
- Font size
- Level of funding for printing.

Item writers should know from the outset the number of pages in the proposed final test form. If it becomes apparent that the length of the test will be limited, stimulus material as well as diagrams and other illustrations should be limited. Irrespective of the amount of space available, the layout of items should be clear and uncluttered.

Booklets of fewer than 20 sides (10 sheets) are usually printed on A4 (210 × 297 millimeters) paper and stapled on one side. Larger booklets tend to be printed on A3 (420 × 297 millimeters) paper and stapled in the middle.

Booklets with more pages usually allow for a wider range of interesting stimulus material and more imaginative items. On the negative side, they cost more to print and distribute. They also take up more storage space for packing and scoring, which can add considerably to overall costs.

Tests are usually printed double-sided. At a minimum, the paper quality needs to be sufficient to ensure that items printed on one side of the page do not bleed through or interfere with the legibility of items printed on the other side of the same page.

Photographs require higher-quality paper for clear reproduction. Finely detailed diagrams also require high-grade paper.

If students are required to write in the test booklets, the paper should be strong enough for them to write their responses without tearing the paper and to write on either side of the same page without the writing showing through.

The cover paper is sometimes of higher quality than that used in the remainder of the test booklet, but this tends to add to costs and is not usually necessary.

Printing booklets for different grade levels in different-colored inks is often useful. It helps ensure that the correct booklets are given to the appropriate students. The ink colors chosen should be easy to read.

A highly experienced proofreader should review the final forms. It is also worth asking competent colleagues who have not been involved in the test development to read the final form to check that it makes sense from a test user's point of view.

There are two critical periods for proofreading the final test forms. After the final forms have been assembled, they should be proofread by the test development manager, by the appropriate item writers, and finally by a professional proofreader. The item writers should check corrections made by the proofreader. Final forms must be proofread a second time when the printer returns the "blues" for checking. The blues are images of the test pages as the printer will reproduce them. The printer will normally return blues within a few days of receiving a test. The test development manager may accept responsibility for proofreading the blues or may prefer to employ a professional proofreader to carry out this task. At least two weeks should be allowed for proofreading and correction of final forms. More time may be required depending on the availability of staff members to make the corrections to booklets.

Proofreaders often find hundreds of small errors, especially in inconsistent use of capitals, punctuation, formatting, layout, and incorrect spelling. If the proofreading of pretests has been thorough and extensive and if minimal substantive changes have been made to the items, then, in theory, proofreading of final forms should reveal few, if any, errors. In practice, this rarely happens. Errors can emerge in the final forms where no errors appeared before. Proofreaders usually need several days to thoroughly proofread final test forms and administration guidelines, even when pretests had been previously proofread.

Place orders for large print jobs with printers several weeks or even months in advance. The printer will advise on the turnaround time. The national assessment team can sometimes negotiate price incentives for early delivery and disincentives or penalties for late delivery.

Printers can make errors in printing test booklets. The most common error is for some pages to be missing in some of the booklets. The test development manager should randomly check boxes of the printed final test booklets for any errors.

HAND-SCORING TEST ITEMS

The national assessment team must ensure that raters who are hand-scoring the final test forms are trained. By this stage, the scoring guides or rubrics—having been revised during pretesting—should be almost final. Before final hand-scoring commences, item writers might select a small sample of completed final test forms, check the clarity and effectiveness of the scoring guides, and possibly make minor revisions.

Setting up a rating center for hand-scoring and establishing effective hand-scoring processes need to be planned well in advance. The national assessment team should have addressed the following questions before hand-scoring begins:

- Where will test materials be stored?
- How will they be taken to the rating centers?
- How will security of test materials be guaranteed? (Tests and scoring guides should not leave the room.)
- What is the timetable for hand-scoring? Will scoring be organized in daily units, in shifts (including an evening shift)? Will raters work on weekends?
- How will raters record data?

- What rating equipment is required? Red or green pens are often preferred because scores in these colors can be seen clearly in the student booklets. Sticky flags or stick-it notes are useful for flagging items that raters have queries about.
- Will raters be paid by number of scripts completed or by amount of time spent rating? Both methods have advantages and disadvantages. In the former, raters may rush and become careless as they try to score as many scripts as possible. In the latter, raters may not apply themselves fully, and their output may be low. A suitable compromise might be to pay by time but to expect a minimum number of scripts to be completed each day.

The staff members needed in a rating center are a chief rater, leading raters, and raters. Those responsible for selecting raters should interview candidates and check their references.

The *chief rater* is responsible for all day-to-day operations. He or she ensures that raters work to schedule, resolves any rating issues, oversees the management of quality control procedures, and maintains test security. The chief rater should be an experienced rater with established operations management skills who is prepared to dismiss staff members who prove unsatisfactory.

The *leading raters* are responsible for monitoring the rating of a particular subject area and implementing quality control procedures. Each test should have at least one leading rater (for example, a leading rater for mathematics and leading rater for reading). The leading raters should be expert in a subject area, have rating experience, and command respect.

The *raters* score the students' responses. Usually, teachers are good raters. Raters should be diligent, consistent, and reliable; they should know their subject area.

The test development manager usually nominates senior item writers from relevant subject areas to train raters. Preferably, the person training raters has also been extensively involved in the development of items and rating guides. The person training the raters should be an expert in the relevant subject. The test development manager might take on the role of training raters in his or her subject area. Ideally, the person who conducted rater training for the pretests should also conduct it for the final forms.

Sufficient time should be allowed for several periods of rater training for each group of raters. Training should emphasize that raters will be required to read a range of possible correct answers. Some of these answers may not be what the rater is used to, may bear little resemblance to textbook answers, or may be poorly expressed or use unconventional vocabulary. Rater training should cover the following points:

- Raters have little or no freedom in determining the appropriateness of a response; there is no room for personal opinions or preferences.
- Students should not be penalized for spelling or grammatical errors in reading, mathematics, or science unless the student's work is impossible to decipher.
- Raters must seek the leading rater's advice when they are not sure how to score a particular response.
- Raters should use the same score (usually 0) consistently for all incorrect responses and all illegible, unintelligible responses, including writing even a single letter or scrawling a single line.
- Raters should use the same scoring code (usually 9) consistently to show that the student made no attempt to answer the item—that is, no pencil mark whatsoever appears in the space provided for the answer.
- To facilitate data entry, raters should use only the space provided in the test booklet when hand-scoring.
- Raters should not be responsible for combining scores to give overall totals.

In training, the emphasis should be on ensuring that raters understand what the scoring task entails and on achieving consistency in scoring. Training methods tend to vary. The following is one suggested method, but many others exist.

- The trainer asks raters to answer each hand-scored item in the test. This process familiarizes raters with the items and ensures that they have properly read and understood them.
- The trainer gives each rater four or five completed test booklets. The trainer discusses the first item and the scoring guide and then raters score this item in their test booklets. The trainer encourages the group to discuss any discrepancies or uncertainties about how

to score a response. Raters are encouraged to share responses that may vary from the examples in the scoring guide. After the first item has been adequately discussed, the trainer moves on to the next item and its scoring guide. This method of training usually takes several hours.

- Raters have a second training session in which they work in pairs. They score some tests individually and then check each other's work and discuss where they vary in their judgments. If they cannot reach agreement, they should consult with the trainer. After the training sessions are over, the leading rater assumes responsibility for the management of the raters. The leading rater should inform the trainer if any issues arise during the scoring of tests.
- During the actual scoring of test booklets, the leading rater should select a few problematic items each day and hold short discussions on them to maintain focus and consistency.

Quality checking short-response items for a national assessment might include an initial rechecking of close to 100 percent of all test booklets. Usually, the leading raters do the checking. They can gradually reduce the rechecking process to 10 to 20 percent of test booklets as raters become consistent and reliable in their scoring.

If a large group of raters is employed, several leading raters will be needed to ensure the quality of checking and to provide prompt feedback to raters about any errors they are making. The leading rater should require raters to rescore items in earlier scored test booklets where they have made scoring mistakes. Procedures for discrepancy rating also should be clarified. Usually, the leading rater's score is the one that counts.

A language test might include one or more items that require an essay-type response. Essays are often double-scored. The second rater scores the essay without knowing the mark or grade assigned by the first rater. The two scores are then compared. Usually, differences of one score point are accepted, and the two scores are averaged. Greater differences between raters' scores require that at least one of the scores be altered. This change might be based on a discussion between both raters. If raters cannot reach agreement, the issue should be referred to the leading rater for adjudication.

Hand-scoring requires intense concentration. Raters should not work for too long in any one day or for too long without a break. A work period of six to six and one-half hours per day is often considered a maximum. A workday might consist of a morning session of three hours with a short break and an afternoon session of three hours with a short break. Slower workers may require an extra half hour or so to complete the expected number of tests per day. Raters should be required to complete daily attendance sheets.

PART 2

CONSTRUCTING QUESTIONNAIRES

CHAPTER 8

DESIGNING QUESTIONNAIRES

A questionnaire is a set of items designed to obtain information from a person. The kind of information can vary widely and may include data on personal characteristics; data on work qualifications and practices; data on working conditions and resources; or background information about the person and his or her attitudes, beliefs, or opinions on certain issues.

A national assessment seeks to obtain a reliable estimate of student achievement (measured in a specially designed test) and information (measured in a questionnaire) about key variables associated with differences in achievement. Tests collect information about student performance, and questionnaires—when used in conjunction with the tests—collect data about variables that might be associated with, or help explain, differences in levels of student performance. For example, questionnaire data can suggest that schools with no libraries are associated with poor student performance or that schools where teachers regularly participate in professional development programs are associated with high student performance. These data suggest ways in which educational resources might be usefully directed to improve student learning.

A good questionnaire collects data about variables for which policy makers want accurate information, variables that they can possibly affect and are willing to influence, and variables that research evidence indicates can affect student achievement.

A common mistake in designing questionnaires is to collect too much information. Policy makers are generally interested in information about only a few key variables. Moreover, even when good scientific reasons may exist for collecting some kinds of data, consideration of the political and social consequences of collecting the data might indicate that a national assessment is not the most appropriate mechanism for doing so.

Information can often be collected from sources other than questionnaires in countries that keep accurate and reliable records about characteristics of schools, teachers, and students. It is worthwhile finding out if government records are a useful source of information, because accessing such records may be cheaper and easier than administering questionnaires.

The questionnaire design should clearly describe what kinds of data will be collected, how the data will be analyzed and reported, and how findings might contribute to improving education. The main steps in questionnaire design are the following:

- Decide what the purpose of a questionnaire is and how the data will be used.
- Develop a blueprint that specifies respondents, focus areas, item types, and coding or scoring and administration protocol (to be completed by an interviewer or to be self-completed).
- Write items, using groups (or panels) of knowledgeable individuals to review and refine items, and design the layout of the form so that it is easy for respondents to use and data entry people can process data efficiently.
- Specify a data analysis plan for processing information collected and creating measurement variables and indicators for subsequent statistical analysis.
- Pretest or field-test questionnaires to establish the suitability of items and response categories.
- Analyze the pretest questionnaire data, refine questionnaires, and produce the final questionnaires for administration.

Table 8.1 provides details of the steps in questionnaire development and the people involved.

TABLE 8.1

Components of Questionnaire Development

Component	Description	People involved
1. Purpose	Clarify the purpose and potential use of the questionnaire data.	Policy makers, key stakeholders, and test development manager
2. Blueprint	Design the questionnaire blueprint to specify respondents, focus areas, item types, coding, and administration protocol.	Test development manager, subject experts, data analyst, experienced item writers, experienced teachers, policy makers, and key stakeholders
3. Items	Write questionnaire items.	Test development manager and item writers
	Refine for clarity and usefulness in questionnaire panels.	Test development manager and item writers
	Review questionnaires.	Test development manager, policy makers, and key stakeholders
4. Data analysis plan	Specify the plan for processing information, for creating measurement variables and indicators, and for types of analysis.	Data analyst and test development manager
5. Pretest	Design, produce, and proofread questionnaires for pretesting.	Test development manager; item writers, design and layout professionals, and proofreaders
	Write administration instructions for pretesting of questionnaires, and train administrators.	Test development manager and item writers
	Pretest questionnaires at the same time that tests are being pretested.	Test development manager, logistics manager, and test administrators
6. Final questionnaire	Analyze pretest questionnaire data.	Test development manager and data analyst
	Refine questionnaire and administration instructions on basis of pretest data and feedback from pretest administrator.	Test development manager, item writers, and data analyst
	Produce final form of questionnaire.	Test development manager, item writers, design and layout professional, and proofreaders

Source: Authors' representation.

Questionnaires and instructions for their administration should be prepared and pretested or field-tested at the same time as the tests. Thus, questionnaire blueprints should be developed at the same time as the test blueprints, and questionnaires should be written and paneled at the same time that test items are being written and paneled.

QUESTIONNAIRE CONTENT

A questionnaire should collect information about key variables that might help explain differences in the performance of students on an achievement test. However, myriad intertwining variables can conceivably affect students' performance. A questionnaire can focus on only a few.

Policy makers usually want to know about variables that are associated with important educational issues in their country, such as the language of instruction, disparities in the distribution of educational resources, or attitudes toward the education of girls. Possibly, policy makers will not know what variables to investigate. They may give a long list of variables that are drawn from personal experience and observation or that they think "ought" to be in a questionnaire. Such a list needs to be reduced to a few focused requirements that are likely to be of use in shaping the content of the questionnaire.

Policy makers may not be aware that the process of analyzing and reporting questionnaire data is expensive and requires technical expertise. Because resources are invariably limited, questionnaires need to be concise and highly relevant. Data collected must also be technically acceptable if they are to be used to explain student performance. Models used by other national assessments may provide a rough guide. Each country has its own needs, however, and these must determine the appropriate nature of the questionnaire.

The test development manager or the person responsible for production of the questionnaire may need to give policy makers some guidance about key variables that are likely to provide useful information. To do so, he or she may need to present policy makers with relevant examples to help them consider how they might use the information collected. This information will help further refine the list of variables to be addressed.

Because questionnaires will be designed to address topics that respondents are likely to know about, the topics will vary for students, parents, teachers, and head teachers. The following sections suggest suitable topics for questionnaires for each of these groups.

Student Questionnaires

Student questionnaires may collect the following information:

- Gender, age, and language background (all usually collected on the front of the test booklet)
- Educational background, such as years at school and periods away from school
- Opportunities to attend school
- Expectations of success and personal or family attitudes about the value of school
- Perceptions of classroom environments, such as sense of safety, friendliness of other students, or support from teachers.

Parent Questionnaires

Parent questionnaires may collect the following information:

- Nationality, gender, and language background
- Home environment, such as access to books, desks, and lights
- Family background, such as education of parents and language spoken at home
- Attitudes toward education, such as commitment to sending children to school, perceptions of the value and relevance of education, or perceptions of the quality of education
- Attention to homework and study resources provided at home for children
- Affordability and accessibility of education for children
- Expectations of educational achievement for children
- Involvement with schools, such as participation in the classroom or on committees
- Nature of school reports about children's progress and their value
- Financial support for school in the form of payment for textbooks and fees.

Teacher Questionnaires

Teacher questionnaires may collect the following information:

- Gender and age
- First language
- Teaching conditions, such as class size, access to resources, percentage of students who have textbooks, access to replacement teachers when sick, and assistance with challenging students
- Educational experience, teacher qualifications, and number of years in this school
- Professional engagement with learning, such as access to and interest in professional development, interest in teaching, and time spent preparing for classes
- Availability of instructional support through classroom visits by head teachers, school inspectors, or supervisors
- Teaching methodology, such as language of instruction, use of assessment, and style of teaching
- Satisfaction with working conditions, such as tenure, rates of pay, and level of supervision
- Relationship with the school community, such as interactions with parents, involvement in school committees, and participation in local community events
- Distance from teacher's home to school.

Head-Teacher Questionnaires

Questionnaires for head teachers may collect the following information:

- Gender and age
- Educational and management experience and qualifications
- School environment, such as quality of buildings and facilities, as well as availability of resources
- School records, such as fluctuations in student numbers, the extent of student or teacher absenteeism, and the frequency of students changing schools
- Professional engagement with school leadership, such as access to and interest in professional development and interest in education

- Leadership style and use of time
- Satisfaction with working conditions, such as tenure, rates of pay, and level and frequency of supervision
- Relationship with school community, such as interactions with parents and participation in local community events.

QUESTIONNAIRE BLUEPRINT

A blueprint is required to guide the development of a questionnaire. It describes the key policy issues that will provide the focus of the questionnaire; identifies the respondents; lists key variables to be addressed; and specifies the format of items, the kinds of response categories, and the administration protocol.

Box 8.1 provides an example of the blueprint of a questionnaire used to collect information about students' values and attitudes toward school and their local community. Recent reforms in education and new curriculum materials being introduced to schools had emphasized teaching students to value their local community and to acquire skills that would assist them in constructively contributing to village life as adults. Papua New Guinea's policy makers wanted to collect information about students' expectations and perceptions of school and the community. The questionnaire was administered to all the students who took the national assessment tests.

QUESTIONNAIRE ITEMS

Several considerations must be taking into account when deciding on the number of items in a questionnaire, including the amount of time available to answer questions, the resources available for analysis, and the complexity of the analysis required. A short, limited questionnaire that is properly analyzed and provides useful information is preferable to a long, comprehensive one that is never fully processed.

The number of items needed to measure a specific variable depends on the nature of the variable. Some variables, such as gender or age, can be measured directly. Others, such as socioeconomic status, tend

BOX 8.1

Attitudes and Values Questionnaire Blueprint

Part I

Focus areas	Attitudes toward school	Beliefs about life in Papua New Guinea	Perceptions of local community
Number of questions	10	15	15
Respondents	Grade 3 Grade 5 Grade 8	Grade 5 Grade 8	Grade 5 Grade 8
Response categories	Yes or no	Yes or no	Yes or no

Part II

Attitudes toward school	Beliefs about life in Papua New Guinea	Perceptions of local community
Beliefs about personal achievement, intended length of schooling, and personal future plans	Attitudes toward education: teaching in vernacular, compulsory education, role of school, education of girls, and roles of women	Perceived level of cooperation in the local community: support for school, local involvement in community events, and sharing of resources
Perceptions of helpfulness of teachers, friendliness of students, bullying, and willingness to make friends from outside village	Attitudes toward community: personal intention to stay in local community or reasons for going	Perceived attitude of local community toward girls and women

Part III

Values	Beliefs about life in Papua New Guinea	Perceptions of local community
Values about conflict resolution	Attitudes toward conflict resolution and fighting	Perceived level of constructive employment in local community and use of peaceful means to resolve problems
Values about personal hygiene habits	Attitudes toward alcohol and drugs	Perceptions of problems caused by drug and alcohol use in local community

Source: Papua New Guinea Department of Education 2004.

to be constructed from several items, such as level of parental education, job status, location of home, and ownership of property. A *raw variable* is the data derived from a direct measure. An *aggregated variable* combines data from two or more items to represent a construct. Policy makers generally find results of analysis based on raw variables easier to interpret than results based on aggregated variables.

Decisions about whether a raw or aggregated variable is needed to support a construct should be based on good research practice and conditions in the country. Both national and international surveys have used aggregated variables. In one international study , for example, the two variables "reading for a utilitarian purpose" and "reading for enjoyment" were based on aggregated variables (see table 8.2).

TABLE 8.2

Functions of Reading in an International Study: Weights Used to Create Two New Variables, "Reading for a Utilitarian Purpose" and "Reading for Enjoyment"

Item (abbreviated)	Weights	
	Utilitarian purpose	Enjoyment
Helps me at school.	0.75	
Helps me pass examinations.	0.74	
Helps me with later school subjects.	0.73	
Helps me work better.	0.65	
I can go to college.	0.65	
Helps me get a good job.	0.63	
My parents think it is important.	0.58	
I get enjoyment.		0.76
It is exciting.		0.72
It is interesting.		0.71
It is like going into another world.		0.68
Nice to think about things I read.		0.54
Fun to think I am a person in a story.		0.53
Nice to do alone.		0.53
Helps me relax.		0.50

Source: Data extracted from Greaney and Neuman 1990 (table 8, loadings less than 0.20 excluded).

Country-specific issues are relevant in deciding how many items are needed to measure a variable. For example, in a country where conditions of teacher education are fairly uniform and all teachers have at least two or three years of tertiary education in recognized institutions, a single raw variable measuring years of tertiary education may be sufficient. In a country where conditions of teacher education vary widely, the quality of teaching institutions is uneven, and many teachers may have been given on-the-job training, however, a number of raw variables may need to be aggregated to represent a construct of teacher education that adequately reflects the situation. Similarly, in a wealthy country, study resources at home may be measured by a single raw variable regarding access to the Internet, but in a poor country, study resources at home may be better represented as an aggregate of raw variables including access to a desk, a chair, a lamp, pencils, paper, and textbooks.

Decisions about whether to use a single raw variable or an aggregated variable to obtain a measure also depend on beliefs about the significance of the possible raw variables. For example, in measuring teaching experience, if its quality varies extensively depending on where teachers are employed, and if there is a belief that location of previous teacher employment might also affect student performance, then information about where the teacher has worked should be collected as well as information about the length of time spent teaching. If there is a belief that the number of years of teaching experience might affect students' performance, regardless of where teachers gained this experience, then a single raw variable is probably sufficient.

ITEM FORMAT

Forced-choice items are a great deal easier, faster, and cheaper to process than open-ended items. Because forced-choice items provide a limited number of categories from which to select a response, data processing is simply a matter of entering the respondent's selection in a computer. Responses to open-ended items, in contrast, have to be processed by hand before they can be entered in a computer.

Questionnaire data are often summarized for reporting. For example, responses to a question about the time students take to travel to school each day may be categorized into a few large bands, such as less than one hour, between one and two hours, and more than two hours. In an open-ended version of this item, some students will give times in minutes and others in hours, others may write "a long time," and still others will give an illegible answer. The range of responses will be large, and categorizing responses will necessarily involve an element of subjectivity, including making decisions about how to classify responses such as "a long time."

Forced-choice items are preferred if a good guess can be made about the likely range and differences in the categories of most respondents' answers. If there is some uncertainty, however, then more finely differentiated categories may be used than are required for reporting purposes. After data are entered, decisions can be made about which categories give little information and which can be combined or dropped (for example, if no one selected them).

Using open-ended items may be feasible if the questionnaire is being administered to a small sample and resources are available to classify the responses by hand. Pretesting or field-testing items as open ended is sometimes useful in providing information to generate categories for a forced-choice version of items in the final administration.

LANGUAGE OF THE QUESTIONNAIRE

The language used in a questionnaire should be a language that respondents are most likely to be able to read and write fluently. However, language choice needs to be balanced with economies of scale. Generally, questionnaires are administered in the same language as the test material.

RESPONDENTS

Given that some background information about students is always collected on the front page of test booklets, the selection of questionnaire respondents depends on what policy makers want to know and the feasibility of obtaining this information reliably and efficiently.

The following are some problems that may be associated with respondents:

- Students may be too young to fill in a questionnaire reliably or accurately.
- Lack of resources may limit the administration of questionnaires to a small group, such as teachers or head teachers, rather than to thousands of students.
- Many parents may be illiterate or unreliable in returning questionnaires.
- Teachers and head teachers may not be motivated to fill in a long questionnaire, or they may feel too threatened to answer questions honestly.

Whatever decision is made about respondents, the sample selected for a questionnaire should be representative of the population. If the questionnaire is being administered to students, the sample that was drawn for the test should respond to the questionnaire. Sampling experts should be consulted about required sample sizes for administration to teachers, head teachers, and parents.

QUESTIONNAIRE ADMINISTRATION

Questionnaires are typically responded to in writing or are administered in an interview. The latter requires a trained interviewer to ask the questions and to write down interviewee responses (perhaps applying codes provided in the questionnaire form).

In large-scale assessments, most questionnaires are written and administered in groups to minimize cost. Questionnaires should contain instructions on how questions should be answered. The instructions might include reasons for collecting the information.

Collection of questionnaire data may be done under the supervision of a fieldworker, who collects the forms after respondents have completed them.

DATA ANALYSIS PLAN

A data analysis plan specifies what kind of information will be provided by each item in a questionnaire and how the information will be used in analysis. The provision of expert statistical assistance in designing the plan will increase confidence that data can be analyzed meaningfully and that the findings will be rigorous and defensible (see volume 4, *Analyzing Data from a National Assessment of Educational Achievement*).

The plan should show the following:

- The measurement characteristics of the variables. The way questionnaire data can be analyzed depends on the measurement characteristics of variables. Numerals attached to nominal or categorical variables (for example, gender) are really only labels and can be used only to distinguish between groups. Numerals attached to ordinal scales (for example, to represent responses to a questionnaire indicating degree of agreement with a statement) provide information on relative values, although they are often treated in statistical analysis as if they possessed the properties of interval (for example, temperature) or ratio scales (for example, number of years of teaching experience).
- How data from a number of variables will be aggregated to produce a new variable, and how the new variable will be used. For example, an index of poverty might be constructed from variables such as household income, location of home, number of rooms in the home, home possessions, number of children, and parents' level of education. How the variables will be aggregated to represent poverty should be considered in the design plan.

CHAPTER 9

ITEM WRITING FOR QUESTIONNAIRES

It should be clear from the way an item is constructed what information is required. Furthermore, respondents should be able to provide the information. Thus, one would not ask young students to recall how many days they had been absent during the school year, because they would be unlikely to be able to do so reliably. At best, they might remember how many days they were away during the previous week.

The wording in items should be as simple and as clear as possible. Vocabulary should be familiar, and sentences should be short and direct. Unless the questionnaire is orally administered, all the respondents should be able to read the questionnaire. It is also important that all respondents interpret questionnaire items in the same way. Otherwise, interpreting results in a meaningful way will be difficult.

The first part of a questionnaire item can be a question, an incomplete sentence, or a statement that respondents evaluate.

The style in which the respondent is addressed should be consistent. Either of the following may be used:

- Refer to "you"; for example, "How old are you?"
- Refer to "I"; for example, "I come to school by …"

QUESTIONS

Questions should be clear and unambiguous. The following question is ambiguous.

How long have you been a teacher?

This question confuses the time that has elapsed since training with the time engaged in teaching. Anyone who has left teaching and returned, such as women who took time out to raise their families, will be unsure how to answer the question. Whether this question is a measure of teacher experience or of time elapsed since training is unclear. There are at least two questions here:

When did you complete your teacher training?
How many years of teaching experience do you have?

The second question is still problematic because it is not clear how years of teaching experience might be measured. For example, should five years' experience, working part time, one day a week, be counted as five years or as the equivalent of one year? If almost all teaching positions in the country are full time, then ambiguity is unlikely, but if many positions are part time, it is. The question might read:

How many years of full-time (or equivalent full-time) teaching experience do you have?

It may be necessary to define what is meant by "equivalent."

STATEMENTS

Items that open with a statement usually require respondents to make some kind of evaluation of the statement, such as "strongly agree," "agree," "disagree," or "strongly disagree."

Negative statements, such as "I do not like school," should be avoided because they can be confusing. If asked to agree or disagree, students who do like school should select a "disagree" category. Young children often find double negatives difficult.

Keep statements as neutral as possible. A statement that says, "I like school" is better than one that says, "I love school." Students can express greater fondness for school by selecting "strongly agree" for their response.

Statements should focus on one issue. Thus, statements such as "I work hard and do well in my schoolwork" should be avoided. Students who do well at school without working hard will not know which response to select. Students who work hard may strongly agree with this statement, although they may not do well in their schoolwork. The statement is better expressed as two statements: "I work hard at school"; "I do well in my schoolwork."

RESPONSE CATEGORIES

Good response categories have the same meaning for all respondents. The following response categories are likely to have different meanings for different people:

How many books are in the class library?
A. none
B. a few
C. some
D. many

The response categories for the item should be quantified so that the meaning is clear:

How many books are in the class library?
A. no library
B. 1 to 10
C. 11 to 20
D. more than 20

Sometimes response categories may have a different meaning for different respondents, but this difference is part of the information sought, as the following item shows:

How good is your school library?
A. no library
B. poor
C. adequate
D. good
E. excellent

If the item is about the respondent's level of satisfaction with the school library, regardless of any objective measure of its quality, then it is a good item. If the item is combined with items that quantify—for example, approximately how many shelves of books or computer facilities are in the library—then the respondent's perception can be compared with more objective measures of the extent of the library facilities.

Response categories need to take into account the level of accuracy of answers that respondents are likely to be able to give. Respondents are unlikely to know the number of books in a library with any kind of accuracy, unless it is very small.

Response categories need to cover all possible responses. If there are a few major categories and many minor ones, listing the major ones and including an option of "other" is preferable. Pretesting helps identify the major categories.

Response categories should not overlap or leave gaps. Both mistakes are shown in the following question:

How long have you been teaching at this school?
A. fewer than 5 years
B. fewer than 10 years
C. more than 10 years

Teachers with fewer than 5 years' teaching experience do not know if they should select the first or the second option. Teachers with 10 years' teaching experience do not have an option to select.

Questionnaire items that open with a statement that respondents are asked to evaluate may have many different response categories. It is important that the categories do not overlap. Some examples of response categories that have been used in the teacher questionnaire for the Trends in International Mathematics and Science Study are

- Yes, no
- Strongly agree, agree, disagree, strongly disagree
- Almost every day, once or twice a week, once or twice a month, never or hardly ever
- Not at all, a little, quite a lot, a great deal
- Not important, somewhat important, very important.

MANAGING SENSITIVE ISSUES

Some issues are sensitive, such as whether teachers have a second job to supplement their salaries. If most respondents are unlikely to answer a question honestly, it should be left out. Policy makers may be very interested in this information, but there is little point in collecting unreliable data. Sometimes, related information that is not as sensitive may be collected instead.

Including questions about sensitive issues may offend respondents who may refuse to answer the rest of the items or to return the questionnaire. If there is concern about the sensitivity of issues, the preferable course is to leave them out.

QUESTIONNAIRE LAYOUT

Two considerations are critical in the layout and design of questionnaires: (a) ease of use for the respondent and (b) ease of use for data processing. Questionnaires are easy to use when they have the following characteristics:

- A simple, consistent way of answering questions
- An uncluttered presentation
- Easily identifiable separate questions
- Response categories that are clearly associated with each question
- Headings, fonts, and layout that are consistent
- Response categories coded for data entry.

Response categories can be set out in many ways. They may be in a vertical column or in a horizontal row. Respondents may circle an

---

BOX 9.1

Poor Alignment of Boxes and Response Categories

The following example shows a poor alignment of boxes and response categories:

How long does it take you to get to school most days?

less than 15 minutes ☐	15 minutes ☐	30 minutes ☐
45 minutes ☐	1 hour ☐	more than 1 hour ☐

The boxes are placed between the response categories instead of being clearly aligned with just one category.

Source: Authors.

BOX 9.2

Better Alignment of Boxes and Response Categories

The following example shows a good alignment of boxes and response categories:

How often do the following people help you with your school homework?

	Never or hardly ever	A few times a year	About once a month	Several times a month	Several times a week
a) Your mother	☐	☐	☐	☐	☐
b) Your father	☐	☐	☐	☐	☐
c) Your brothers and sisters	☐	☐	☐	☐	☐
d) One of your grandparents . . .	☐	☐	☐	☐	☐

Source: Authors.

---

alphabet letter or a number, or they may tick a box to indicate their selection. Consistency in the style of response is preferable.

An example is provided in box 9.1 of an item in which responses are not clearly identified with response categories. Box 9.2 shows a better alignment.

REVIEWING QUESTIONNAIRES

Writing questionnaires is much more difficult than it looks. All items must be carefully scrutinized and revised to ensure that they are clear and unambiguous. Asking a panel to review the questionnaire is strongly recommended. Members of the panel should include item writers, someone familiar with the characteristics of the respondent population, and someone who is able to ensure that the items are culturally appropriate. Some national and international assessments now check how respondents interpret items before the main administration of the questionnaire.

It is useful if panel members attempt to complete the questionnaire as though they were respondents. This process will help identify where categories of response might be unclear, might overlap, or might fail to include some kinds of response.

Panel members should critique the items, especially for clarity of wording and suitability of response categories. They should ensure that wording is as simple and clear as possible, that the style of items is consistent, and that items are presented in a logical order with appropriate instructions.

Panel members should check that items match the questionnaire blueprint and ensure that each item provides the required information. They also need to check that the number of items used is appropriate for measuring each variable with sufficient precision.

After the questionnaire has been refined, policy makers should be given the opportunity to review it. Policy makers need to approve the items, especially if they touch on politically sensitive issues. Policy makers also need to check that the items will provide useful information.

After questionnaires have been refined, they should be pretested or field-tested along with the test materials. Pretesting provides the opportunity to improve the quality of items and reduce the time and cost of processing data from the final questionnaire. Items that do not work (for example, where respondents are confused) can be dropped, and categories of response can be expanded or contracted.

Following administration of the questionnaire, the administrator should collect feedback from respondents (students or teachers) about items that are unclear or that do not contain appropriate information. Administrators should check that no items are considered offensive because they touch on sensitive issues.

More formal statistical analysis of responses may indicate that response categories need to be more finely differentiated. For example, if most students select a particular response category for an item. The category should be split into more finely differentiated categories to obtain more precise information.

If the range of possible responses to an item is potentially very large and hard to anticipate, the item should be left open-ended in the pretest. Responses can then be classified and used to generate categories for a forced-choice item in the final questionnaire.

The accompanying CD contains examples taken from national and international assessments of questionnaires for students, teacher, school heads, and parents. It also includes examples of scoring guides for open-ended responses.

10

CODING QUESTIONNAIRE RESPONSES

Response categories must be coded for data entry. Coding may be alphabetical or numerical.

Alphabetical codes usually require respondents to circle the letter for their response. This method may not be suitable for younger students. Ticking boxes or shading circles can be an easier way for people with limited literacy skills. If the items use this kind of layout, they should be coded numerically.

If numerical coding is used, the first response category is usually coded 1, the second category is coded 2, and so on. Data entry is more efficient if the codes are printed on the questionnaire. A small grayscale font can be used, as shown in box 10.1. In the example, the response categories are numbered under the boxes: walking is category 1, public transport is category 2, and so on. The student ticks the box that applies to him or her. The data entry person enters the number of the box that the student selected.

If respondents are given the opportunity to select more than one response category for an item, each category should be treated as a separate item for data entry and data processing. This procedure makes keeping track of which categories each respondent selected possible. The item in box 10.2 is presented to the respondent as one

---

BOX 10.1

Grayscale Coding Example

Today I came to school by

walking. ☐   public transport. ☐   private transport. ☐   riding an animal. ☐
1   2   3   4

BOX 10.2

Example Treating Items as Separate Categories for Data Entry

If you were away last week, check one or more boxes to show your reason.

☐ I was sick.
1

☐ I had to help my parents.
1

☐ The weather was bad.
1

☐ I did not have food.
1

☐ My family had problems.
1

☐ I did not have a clean uniform or proper clothes to wear.
1

☐ It was not safe (peace and order problems).
1

☐ Other _____
1

Source: Authors.

---

question with multiple possible responses; however, it is treated as eight separate items in data entry. Responses to the first category (absent through sickness) are recorded as either 1 or missing, responses to the second (helping parents) are recorded as either 1 or missing, responses to the third category (bad weather) are similarly recorded, and so on for each of the eight categories.

PREPARING QUESTIONNAIRES FOR DATA ENTRY

Questionnaire data can be scanned with special equipment or entered manually. The design and layout of the questionnaire has to be customized if machine scanning is to be used.

If data entry is being done manually, information can be entered directly from the questionnaire if response categories have been coded. Data entry people may have difficulty maintaining a high level of accuracy, however, especially if they are unfamiliar with this kind of work. Accuracy is also likely to be compromised if the layout of the items varies extensively or if some items have a large number of response categories.

Data entry will be facilitated if scorers and raters write the code for the selected category in the left-hand margin, next to each item number. Data entry then becomes a simple matter of entering the codes written in the margin. Adding lightly shaded boxes in the margin for scorers and raters to write the codes makes the process more efficient.

CODING MISSING OR AMBIGUOUS RESPONSES

Sometimes respondents do not answer items or answer them ambiguously, such as selecting more than one response category when categories are mutually exclusive.

Collecting information about missing responses indicates whether respondents consistently failed to answer some items. For example, the questionnaire may be too long, so that items at the end are not answered, or an item may be too close to other items and easily overlooked. Collecting information about ambiguous responses will also indicate whether an item is possibly unclear to many respondents or whether the respondents do not understand how to complete the questionnaire.

The data entry person needs to know how to code missing or ambiguous responses. Codes used for missing or ambiguous responses should not be confused with the codes used for categories of response.

A letter of the alphabet may be used to denote missing or no attempt, such as X. The code for ambiguous responses could be a second letter, such as Y. Multiple-choice items on tests use codes of 9 for missing and 8 for selecting two or more options. These codes are usually not used for questionnaires because some questionnaire items will likely have 8 or 9 response categories.

CHAPTER 11

MATCHING QUESTIONNAIRES AND TEST DATA

How questionnaire data and test data are matched will be guided by the needs of analysis and reporting. All matches must be clearly and unambiguously established before data collection. Any matching error discovered after data have been collected may be difficult or impossible to fix. Such errors could result in having to abandon some planned analyses.

STUDENT QUESTIONNAIRES

The easiest way to match student questionnaires and test data is to print the tests and the questionnaires in one booklet. The student records his or her name on the booklet, and the test administrator ensures the student works in his or her own booklet for each of the test sessions.

If the tests and questionnaires are separate documents, one method of matching data is to overprint or label both tests and questionnaires with the students' names. Names are taken from the school roll and should be identical for each label. Again, the test administrator needs to ensure that students work on tests and questionnaires bearing their clearly labeled names.

If separate booklets and questionnaires cannot be prelabeled, the student questionnaires need to have sufficient identifying information to allow them to be matched with test data. It is preferable to allocate a numerical identity (ID) to students and to ensure that they use the same ID number on each booklet and questionnaire. The test administrator will have to oversee this procedure. The data analyst will also need the list of student names and ID numbers, because names may be matched as a backup when ID errors occur.

Reliance on students' names to match forms is not desirable. Unless names are absolutely identical on each form and are entered identically by the data processing person, with no spelling errors, the computer cannot match them. Matching will then have to be done manually, a time-consuming and expensive exercise. Some students will make matching by names additionally complicated by using different names (such as shortened forms, family names, or religious names) on different forms; by writing illegibly on one or more forms; or by failing to write their name on one or more forms.

PARENT QUESTIONNAIRES

Parent questionnaire data are usually matched with student data. The matching will probably be done through the students' names. The same problems apply as outlined for student questionnaires. Procedures should be set up to ensure consistency.

TEACHER AND HEAD-TEACHER QUESTIONNAIRES

Teacher and head-teacher questionnaires are usually matched with the grade and the school only. If the students' grade is known, the teacher information can be used in the analysis of student data. The test administrator should check that teachers and head teachers have provided this information on the questionnaire.

When questionnaires are returned from schools, each school's questionnaires should be stored in a separate bundle. Thus, even if the school information was not supplied on some questionnaires, relevant information can be obtained from other questionnaires in the same bundle.

PART 3

DESIGNING A
MANUAL FOR TEST
ADMINISTRATION

CHAPTER 12

THE TEST ADMINISTRATORS' MANUAL

A manual is required to guide test administration, which must be standardized so that all students take the test under the same conditions. The main purpose of the manual is to specify the exact conditions under which a test must be conducted, including preparation requirements and procedures for ensuring test security. Students taking the test must work through the same practice questions and receive the same instructions about how to show their answers. All must be given the same amount of time to do the test with the same degree of supervision.

Students' performance on a national assessment should be a measure of their ability to answer the items without external support. The students should understand what they have to do and how to show their answers, but they should not be given any other assistance or have access to any resources that are not a part of the test. Following the procedures laid down in an administration manual should help ensure that this will be the case. The accompanying CD contains examples of test administration and school coordination manuals.

CONTENTS OF THE MANUAL

Administration manuals should provide information answering each of the following questions:

- *What is the test for?*
  - Brief explanation of the purpose of the test and the way the data will be used

- *Which tests are given, which students are tested, and when are they tested?*
  - Which tests are being administered in the school
  - Which students should take each test
  - Dates and times of test administration
  - Order of administration of tests
  - Length of time of administration of each test
  - Any required breaks between test administrations
  - Any options for flexibility in the administration schedule.

- *What test materials are needed?*
  - List of all the test materials that are supplied
  - Quantities of each test material supplied, such as one per student or one per teacher
  - List of any materials the school needs to provide, such as pencils and erasers.

- *How should the room be set up for the test?*
  - Physical facilities the school needs to provide, such as desks and chairs
  - Resources that might assist students should be removed from the room or covered up, such as charts of multiplication tables or posters displaying grammatical rules.

- *What preparation is required?*
  - How the principal or head teacher might motivate staff members and students to support the administration of the test before the actual administration
  - What information the test administrator might require, such as a class list of names

- How test booklets might need to be sorted, numbered, or named to be ready for use
- How student groups might need to be organized for testing.

- *How should the test be conducted?*
  - How students should write their name on booklets and record background information on the front cover
  - When and how the administrator should check that students have correctly recorded the information on the front cover of the test booklet
  - How the practice questions should be administered and explained
  - What instructions the students should receive about the test
  - What level of support the administrator can offer during the test
  - How long students have to complete the test
  - What conditions the administrator needs to maintain during the test
  - Who should be allowed into the room during test administration.

- *How should test materials be stored?*
  - Procedures to ensure the security of the test materials before, during, and after the test.

- *Who can be contacted for help?*
  - Contact details for people who can assist with problems or provide additional information.

Additional information may be included in the administration manual to streamline the movement of test booklets in and out of schools. This information is likely to vary depending on whether an external agency or teachers in the school administer the tests.

USE OF THE MANUAL

The head teacher or principal of the school and the test administrator both need to use the manual. Some assessments prepare separate manuals for principals or for those who have overall responsibility for carrying out the national assessment activities within individual schools.

The head teacher (or principal) needs the manual to ensure his or her school is appropriately prepared for the test administration. He or she should know enough about the test to encourage the staff and the students to support the administration and to motivate students to try their best. The head teacher (or principal) or national assessment school coordinator (if one has been appointed) should have sufficient information to be able to organize the school and to make sure that the correct students are available at the required time, with the right materials; that they will have adequate space to take the test; and that test materials can be stored securely.

Test administrators need the manual to tell them exactly what they have to do to administer the test properly and when and how to do it. They need to check that sufficient test materials are available and that the correct students have been selected to take the test. They need to know what information to give students about the test, how to explain the practice questions, and how much time students have to do the tests. They also should know what security procedures to use for storing test materials.

FEATURES OF A MANUAL

A good manual contains all necessary information and is easy to use. The information is logically ordered, instructions are clear and complete, and language is simple and direct. Bullet points, boxes, or tables will make the information easier to read. A good manual should have a table of contents with clear headings (see box 12.1).

HOW MUCH DETAIL IS NECESSARY?

Information about the general conditions of test administration and the preparation of test materials should be comprehensive but, at the same time, as brief as possible (see box 12.2).

Instructions that the test administrator gives to students should be written out in full. Anything that the test administrator must tell

BOX 12.1

Administration Manual Instructions

In a national assessment, the following information appeared in a large font (Arial 14 point), taking up the entire opening page of the administration manual:

Please read this Administration Handbook before your students do the test.

Students must do this test over TWO DAYS.

- The test is divided into four sessions. Students must do two sessions each day.
- Students must have a break between each session.
- Do not let students work through the whole test at once.

Administration Rules

- Teachers must supervise all sessions at all times.
- Students must NOT take test booklets out of the classroom or work on them after the teacher has left.
- Students must use the pencils with erasers on the end that have been supplied.
- Students must not use any classroom materials, such as workbooks, dictionaries, or calculators, when they do the tests.
- Students must not be helped with answering the questions. For example, if a student does not understand what to do, explain the practice questions again and tell him/her to try his/her best but do not give any further help.

Test Security

- The test materials must be STORED SECURELY AT ALL TIMES.
- Student test booklets must NOT be copied for any purpose.
- Students must NOT take test booklets home.

Source: Papua New Guinea Department of Education 2004.

students about the test, the practice questions, or the conditions of the test administration should be typed. The test administrator should read from the manual without making any changes to the wording. This procedure ensures that all students taking the test receive exactly the same instructions.

BOX 12.2

Information for Teachers and Principals

Information about the test materials should be concise and listed in a way that is easy to check. The following extract from a large-scale assessment in Papua New Guinea tells the head teacher or principal what materials have been sent to the school and how to find out which classes will participate in the test:

Test Materials

Your Senior Primary School Inspector will tell you which classes in your school need to participate in this test.

You should have received the following materials:

- a cover letter for the head teacher

- a student test booklet for each participating student

- an administration handbook for each teacher administering the test

- a teacher background questionnaire for each participating teacher

- a pencil with an eraser on the end for each participating student

If any materials are missing or you do not have enough materials, please contact your Senior Primary School Inspector.

Source: Papua New Guinea Department of Education 2004.

PRACTICE QUESTIONS

Box 12.3 presents general procedural instructions and a description of the purpose of the practice questions. The instructions that the administrator gives to the students are written out in full and highlighted in a shaded box. The administrator must read these instructions as they are printed. The illustration of money that is part of the practice question in the student booklets is also shown in the administration manual so that the administrator knows what the students are looking at without having to read from the manual and hold a student test booklet open at the same time.

TRYOUT

The manual should be prepared for tryout in the pretest or field test of the test items. Pretesting the manual will highlight any

BOX 12.3

Administration of Practice Items

The following extract shows part of the instructions for the administration of some practice questions:

Day One: Session 1

MATHEMATICS PRACTICE QUESTIONS FOR GRADE 3 (approximately 10 minutes)

Make sure each student has his/her own test booklet with his/her name written on the front cover. The practice questions are provided to show students different ways they will show their answers.

Ask students to open their booklets to the Mathematics Practice Questions (first page).

SAY

We are going to do some mathematics today so we can find out all the different things that you can do in mathematics. First we will do some practice questions so you know what to do and how to show your answers.

Hold up a student booklet and point to the practice questions. Check that everyone has found the right questions.

SAY

Let's look at practice question one. I will read it to you.

Here is a picture of some money.

(continued)

How much money is there altogether?

Is it 2 toea or 7 toea or 25 toea or 205 toea?

Color in the small circle beside the right answer. Color in one circle only.

Wait until all students have finished and then check their answers.

SAY

The answer is 25 toea. You needed to color in the small circle beside 25 toea. If you made a mistake, rub it out and color in the right answer.

Wait until all students have corrected their work if necessary.

Source: Papua New Guinea Department of Education 2004.

misunderstandings or ambiguities that require clarification or refinement in the final version. Because the pretest or field-test conditions should be as similar as possible to those of the final administration, the manual should be in as finished a form as possible at the time of the tryout.

General instructions about the administration of the test can usually be written any time after the blueprints have been finalized. The blueprints should specify all the requirements about the number of tests and their length and about which students should take the test.

During the pretest, the administrator should collect information such as the following to assist the test development manager in refining the final test:

- Whether students needed all the practice questions, whether there were enough practice questions, and whether explanations were sufficiently clear
- Whether the test was the right length or too long, and approximately how many students finished more than 10 minutes early (if different forms are used in the same class, the administrator can compare the length of time students required for each form)
- Whether students appeared to be engaged by the test

- Whether students had adequate and sufficient resources, such as pencils or erasers
- Whether the school facilities were suitable for conducting a test.

REVIEW

The test development manager and the item writers are responsible for the review and refinement of the practice question instructions. The practice questions and administration instructions should be given to the same kind of panel that is set up to review items.

The test development manager and the person responsible for the logistics of test production and distribution should review and refine procedures for the movement of test booklets in and out of schools.

Several people with backgrounds similar to that of the test administrators should also review the entire manual to check that the instructions are clear and to clarify any ambiguities that might arise.

Like all test materials, the manual should be thoroughly and regularly proofread by people who are expert at this task. Instructions for the practice questions and test administration can be properly proofread only if the proofreader also has copies of the relevant student test booklets.

CHAPTER 13

THE TEST ADMINISTRATOR

CHOICE OF TEST ADMINISTRATOR

People should be confident that the test was administered under standardized conditions. Test administrators must be widely regarded as trustworthy.

The choice of test administrator depends on conditions in a country. School inspectors may be ideal administrators in some countries but problematic in others. If the inspectors see test administration as an additional task that is outside their job description, that uses scarce resources, or that is of little interest to them, they may not be motivated to do the job properly.

External administrators are used in some national assessments. Ideally, they are people who can follow instructions precisely, have the time and resources to do the task properly, and have no particular interest in the outcome of the test other than to administer it correctly. In East Timor, for example, census collectors were trained and paid to administer a national assessment in schools. They were people who understood the importance of collecting data in a systematic way and had no investment in students' performance. Their work was supervised to ensure it was of an appropriate standard.

In some countries, administration of a national assessment by teachers would seriously undermine the credibility of the data, but in other countries, it may not. The main problem with asking teachers to administer the test is that they may deliberately or unintentionally offer assistance to students. There are many possible reasons for this phenomenon. Some teachers may worry that the test data will be used to judge their performance as teachers. They may feel that they need to assist students with the test to keep their jobs or to maintain their professional status. Head teachers may feel that their status is even more threatened. Some teachers may feel that the test is an unfair measure of their teaching or of their students' performance and feel obliged to provide assistance to make the test "fair." Some teachers may have every intention of administering the test as instructed but may be unable to let go of their teaching role. They may help students without even being aware of what they are doing or because they cannot bear to see students struggling and not offer assistance.

Volume 3 in this series, *Implementing a National Assessment of Educational Achievement*, addresses the selection of test administrators and outlines some advantages and disadvantages of different types of test administrators.

FOLLOWING INSTRUCTIONS

The manual should distinguish between specific instructions that must be followed to the word from more general instructions that allow the administrator some scope to adapt them to the conditions in the class. The test administrator should not deviate from any specific instructions. Pretesting the manual should help identify any errors or ambiguities in the instructions.

Test administrators should help students only to understand what they have to do and how to show their answers. Test administrators should make clear that they cannot help any students answer questions. They should not offer any assistance in interpreting a question, in explaining the meaning of a word, or in suggesting ways the student might try to answer a question. If a student asks for help, the administrator should tell the student just to try his or her best.

Administrators must not translate into another language for students unless the instructions specifically allow this role.

In some tests, administrators may read the questions to students. The test administrator should read slowly and distinctly the whole test aloud to the class, question by question, or read single questions as requested by the students. In either case, the administrator must read the exact words of the question in the language in which they are printed.

Administrators must have a watch or clock. They should write down on the blackboard or on a paper the precise time the test commences and the time it finishes. Administrators should ensure that students are aware of the time they have to do a test. This usually involves telling students how much time they have at the outset and giving a reminder when the last 10 minutes, last 5 minutes, or last 2 minutes are reached, depending on the length of the test.

Administrators should quietly encourage students to attempt the whole test if they are obviously spending too long on a question and are reluctant to move on. Administrators can do so by simply whispering the suggestion that the student write his or her best answer and then try the next question.

Only materials that are specified in the manual are allowed in the room during test administration. Usually, students bring their own pencils and erasers for a test. Pencil cases and bags should not be allowed. Anything that might assist the students in answering the test questions should be removed from the room. Students should not have access to resources such as dictionaries or calculators unless the test conditions specifically allow their use.

The test administrator, students participating in the test, and possibly a supervisor should be the only people in the room during test administration. The head teacher or principal or other teachers should not be permitted to walk around the room. The test manager should be notified of unavoidable changes in test administration conditions.

During the administration of the test, the administrator should collect information about any variations that occur in the conditions of administration for individual students. Often the front cover of the test booklet will have space for the administrator to indicate that students were absent for all or part of a test. If a student has to leave the room early because of illness and does not complete the test, the administrator should record this information.

The CD that accompanies this book has examples of general and specific instructions for test administrators. It also offers some suggestions on how to lay out a test administration manual.

QUALITY ASSURANCE

Administrators should be selected for their suitability for the task. They should be fluent in the language in which the manual is written. They also should be committed to doing their task well.

Regardless of their levels of seniority or academic qualifications, administrators require training. They should attend a training session that explains the purpose of the test and their role in its administration. They should understand why following instructions is important, and they should be given the opportunity to practice administering the test with fellow test administrators. They should have the opportunity to ask questions about the procedures outlined in the manual.

If teachers are to administer the tests to their own students, the training must ensure that they understand the purpose of the test and are reassured that the data will not be used to judge them. They should understand the importance of not assisting students in answering questions.

Administrators should be supervised for at least some of the time they administer the test. Supervising everyone may not be possible, but random checks of some administrators should be feasible.

Administrators can also be asked to fill in and sign checklists of their tasks to help ensure that they have completed their job.

ADMINISTRATOR'S CHECKLIST

Details of what should be in the administrator's checklist will vary, depending on who is administering the test and the procedures developed for tracking booklets and ensuring security. Box 13.1 provides an example of an administration checklist used in the Philippines. A further example can be seen in volume 3 in this series, *Implementing a National Assessment of Educational Achievement*.

BOX 13.1

Administration Checklist: An Example from the Philippines

The administrator must check every item to show that he or she completed it and sign the form at the end.

Name			Date	
Task		Reference	Time	Completed
1. Complete the student test booklet allocation (STBA) form by inserting the test numbers in consecutive order and entering the students' names in alphabetical order.		STBA form	10 min.	☐
2. Administer teacher questionnaire.		Teacher questionnaire form	15 min.	☐
3. Complete feedback form.		Teacher feedback form	10 min.	☐
4. Distribute the **allocated test to each student** and mark absent against students not in attendance.		STBA form	10 min.	☐
5. Read introduction from *Guidelines*.		*Administrator Guidelines*, p. 7	5 min.	☐
6. Ask students to complete **student details** on front cover of test.		*Administrator Guidelines*, p. 9	5 min.	☐
7. **Check** that **every student** has completed the required student details on front cover.			10 min.	☐
8. Follow instructions for Session 1.		*Administrator Guidelines*, pp. 11–13	60 min.	☐
9. For **breaks**, ask students to leave the room by row and to **leave their test on their desks.**			15 min.	☐
10. Follow instructions for Session 2.		*Administrator Guidelines*, pp. 15–17	60 min.	☐

(continued)

11. For **breaks**, ask students to leave the room by row and to **leave their test on their desks.**		15 min.	☐
12. Follow instructions for Session 3.	*Administrator Guidelines,* pp. 19–21	70 min.	☐
13. Collect all test booklets and check off their return using the STBA form.	STBA form	10 min.	☐
14. **Account for all tests** and make sure every test has been returned.	STBA form	5 min.	☐
15. Dismiss class.		2 min.	☐
16. Sign STBA form.	STBA form	2 min.	☐
17. Collect and pack **all test materials** in the box provided, including i. STBA form ii. Teacher questionnaire iii. Teacher feedback form iv. All completed tests v. All unused tests.		10 min.	☐ ☐ ☐ ☐ ☐
18. Securely store materials		10 min.	☐
19. Return materials to your senior district supervisor (SDS) for the Regional Assessment of Mathematics, Science, and English (RAMSE).	SDS RAMSE distribution form	Travel time	☐
20. Return this completed checklist to your SDS.	RAMSE administrative checklist	2 min.	☐
Administrator signature _____			

Source: Philippine Department of Education 2004.

CHAPTER 14

INFORMING SCHOOLS ABOUT THE NATIONAL ASSESSMENT

Students need to be motivated to try their best on the national assessment. Students are usually best motivated by having teachers explain the purpose of the test to them and by ensuring that they understand that the test results will be used to help improve teaching and not to judge them.

All students need to feel encouraged to participate, especially those with weaker skills. Deciding the best time to inform students of the test dates will depend on circumstances in the school. If students are threatened by a test and may stay away from school, then not telling them exactly when the test will be administered is preferable. If students are excited by the possibility of taking a test and more likely to come to school, then telling them when it will be administered is preferable.

The implementing agency should ensure that schools are informed about the purpose of the test well in advance of the test administration. Information can be provided through seminars, letters, or phone contact. It is advisable to be honest and clear about what data are being collected, how they will be reported and used, and what feedback (if any) the school will receive about students' performance.

Principals and teachers in participating schools should be told that their particular schools and classes have been selected to help gain information about what students do and do not know. The purpose of gathering this information is to help improve the national education system. Individual schools or classes are not being judged in sample-based national assessments. Principals and teachers in participating schools should also be told that all test data and questionnaire responses will be treated as confidential.

Procedures are required to ensure that schools have agreed to participate in the assessment before external administrators are assigned to the school. It is also necessary to ensure that external administrators have all the necessary introductions, such as a letter of endorsement, so that they can be sure the school will support them in meeting their responsibilities. Volume 3, *Implementing a National Assessment of Educational Achievement*, contains further suggestions about informing schools, including a draft letter.

APPENDIX A

GLOSSARY

administration manual: A written set of instructions about how, when, and where tests should be conducted; the manual may also include information about the movement of test booklets in and out of schools.

administrator: A person who supervises the conduct of the test and is responsible for ensuring that the test conditions are standardized according to the administration manual.

aggregate data: Combined data to give an overall score, such as a single score derived from a 30-item test.

answer sheet: A sheet that is separate from the test booklet and used by students to record their responses to test items.

blueprint: Specifications about the criteria that final test items must meet, including the proportion of items to address each aspect of a curriculum area, test length, item format, and any other criteria or constraints regarding test development.

chief rater: The person responsible for management of the rating center and resolution of discrepancies in scores.

circular linking: The linking of a group of test forms from the first form to the last.

classical item analysis: A statistical methodology for the analysis of test data.

closed constructed-response items: Items that require students to generate a short response with a small and finite set of correct answers.

cross-check rating: A review of hand-scores to check that they consistently match the scoring guide score categories; usually the review is done by the leading rater on the spot to give immediate feedback to raters about the quality of their work.

data: Information collected from a test, usually entered into a computer software program.

data analysis: Use of a statistical methodology to analyze and interpret test data.

data analyst: The person responsible for the statistical analysis of data.

dichotomous score: An item that is scored as correct or incorrect, thus having two possible scores, 0 and 1.

discrepancy rating: Procedures for managing disputed scores that arise from cross-checking or double-rating of student-generated responses; usually these procedures are managed by the chief rater.

discriminating items: Items that differentiate between the performances of high- and low-ability students: that is, high-ability students are more likely than are low-ability students to answer the item correctly.

distractors: The incorrect options in a multiple-choice item.

double-rating: A process of rating student-generated responses to items twice; the second rater does not see the first score.

essay: An extended written response to a prompt, usually half a page or more.

field test: Another name for a "trial test" that is conducted before the final test, with a small sample of students, to establish the quality and suitability of items and administration manuals.

final form: The booklets of tests that are administered to a sample population.

framework: A document that defines the purpose of the test and indicates what should be measured, how it should be measured, why it is being measured, and how it should be reported.

full cohort: All the students in the country meeting given criteria, such as being in a particular grade level at a given time.

grayscale: A light gray shade of print.

hand-scoring: The allocation of scores to students' responses to items by human scorers (not machines).

horizontal linking: The linking of items between forms at the same year or grade level.

incorrect responses: Items for which the student's response fits the category for a score of 0.

item: A single part of a test with an individual score; it may be a question, an unfinished sentence, or a single part of a test or questionnaire with an individual score or code.

item panel: A small group consisting of three to six people who critically review and refine all aspects of items to ensure that they are of high quality.

item pool: A collection of items tested in a field trial or pretest and of secure items from previous tests that are suitable for use in future tests.

leading rater: An experienced rater responsible for cross-checking hand-scoring to ensure consistency and reliability of a rater's work.

learning area: A major focus in a curriculum, such as mathematics or science.

linear linking: The linking of a group of test forms from one to the next without the first form being linked back to the last.

link items: Items that are replicated in two or more test booklets to allow data from administration of the booklets to be compared.

longitudinal linking: The linking of test forms over time.

missing responses: Items that the student has made no attempt to answer.

multiple-choice items: Items that require students to select the only correct response to a question from a number of options.

multiple-choice key: The correct option in a multiple-choice item.

open-ended short-response items: Items that require a student to generate a short response, such as one or two sentences or several modifications to a table, chart, or diagram.

partial-credit item: An item that has two or more categories of correct response; these categories are usually hierarchical for items in the final form of the test but may not be hierarchical for pretest, field test, or trial items.

pilot test: Another name for a "trial test" that is conducted before the final test, with a small sample of students, to establish the quality and suitability of items, questionnaires, and administration manuals.

point-biserial correlation: Method used in item analysis to provide a measure of the correlation (relationship) between the score (right or wrong) that students get for an individual item and the overall score they get on the remaining items.

policy makers: Government officials who shape educational policies.

pretest: Another name for a "trial test" that is conducted before the final test, with a small sample of students, to establish the quality and suitability of items, questionnaires, and administration manuals.

proofreading: A detailed review of every aspect of a text to ensure that it is clear, consistent, and free of errors.

random sample: A statistically selected group of students that meets given criteria, including a distribution of key variables that matches the distribution of the same variables in the full cohort.

rater: A person who hand-scores items according to a scoring guide.

rating center: The place where hand-scoring of test items is organized and raters are trained and supervised.

score: Points allocated to a student response on the basis of the categories of a scoring guide.

scoring guides: Descriptions of the scoring categories that are used to classify student-generated responses to items.

secure items: Items that have been kept out of the public domain; they may have been administered in a previous test, but test conditions have prevented duplication or leaking.

standardized conditions: Test conditions that are specified in the administration manual and kept the same for all students to whom the test is administered; all students receive the same amount of support, are given the same instructions, and have the same amount of time to do the test.

stem: The part of a multiple-choice item that precedes the options, usually a question, incomplete sentence, or instruction.

stimulus material: Text, diagrams, or charts that provide the context for one or more items.

substrand: Aspects or groupings within a curriculum learning area; for example, mathematics may be separated into substrands of number, space, pattern, and measurement.

table of specifications: Another name for a blueprint.

test: One or more items that students respond to under standardized conditions; the items are designed to allow students to demonstrate their knowledge, skills, and understandings.

test objectivity: The extent to which the test is unaffected by the choice of task or choice of assessor; that is, the task is fair and inclusive and has clear criteria for making scoring judgments.

test population: The students to whom the test will be administered.

test reliability: The extent to which the evidence collected is sufficient to make generalizations.

test usefulness: The extent to which the test serves its purpose.

test validity: A broad concept that involves making appropriate interpretations and uses of scores or test information.

trial test: Another name for a "pretest" or "field test" that is conducted before the final test, with a small sample of students, to establish the quality and suitability of items, questionnaires, and administration manuals.

unbiased items: Items that are a fair test of achievement and do not give advantage to certain groups on the basis of characteristics that are not relevant to the knowledge or skill being assessed.

unit: A collection of items that is based on a common piece of stimulus material.

vertical linking: The linking of test forms used at different grade levels through the use of common items.

APPENDIX B

FURTHER READING

Allen, N. L., J. R. Donoghue, and T. L. Schoeps. 2001. *The NAEP 1998 Technical Report*. Washington, DC: National Center for Education Statistics.

Australian Council for Educational Research. No date. *Literacy and Numeracy National Assessment* (LANNA), Sample Questions, Numeracy Year 5. http://www.acer.edu.au/documents/LANNA_Y5NumeracyQuestions.pdf.

Baker, F. 2001. *The Basics of Item Response Theory*. College Park, MD: ERIC Clearinghouse on Assessment and Evaluation, University of Maryland.

Beaton, A. E., and E. G. Johnson. 1989. "Overview of the Scaling Methodology used in the National Assessment." *Journal of Educational Measurement* 29: 163–75.

Bloom, B. S., M. D. Engelhart, E. J. Furst, W. H. Hill, and D. R. Krathwohl. 1956. *Taxonomy of Educational Objectives: Handbook 1—Cognitive Domain*. London: Longmans, Green.

Campbell, J. R., D. L. Kelly, I. V. S. Mullis, M. O. Martin, and M. Sainsbury. 2001. *Framework and Specifications for PIRLS Assessment 2001*. Chestnut Hill, MA: International Study Center, Boston College.

Chatterji, M. 2003. *Designing and Using Tools for Educational Assessment*. Boston: Allyn and Bacon.

Educational Research Centre. 1978. *Drumcondra Attainment Tests, Manual, Level II, Form A*. Dublin: Educational Research Centre.

Eivers, E., G. Shiel, R. Perkins, and J. Cosgrove. 2005. *The 2004 National Assessment of English Reading.* Dublin: Educational Research Centre.

Forster, M. 2000. *A Policy Maker's Guide to International Achievement Studies.* Camberwell, Australia: Australian Council for Educational Research.

———. 2000. *A Policy Maker's Guide to Systemwide Assessment Programs.* Camberwell, Australia: Australian Council for Educational Research.

Greaney, V., and S. B. Neuman. 1990. "The Functions of Reading: A Cross-Cultural Perspective." *Reading Research Quarterly* 25 (3):172–95.

Haladyna, T. M. 1999. *Developing and Validating Multiple-Choice Test Items.* 2nd ed. Hillsdale, NJ: Lawrence Erlbaum.

Harlen, W., ed. 2008. *Student Assessment and Testing.* Vols. 1–4. London: Sage

IEA (International Association for the Evaluation of Educational Achievement). 1998. *Third International Mathematics and Science Study—TIMSS Sample Items.* Chestnut Hill, MA: International Study Center, Boston College. http://www.edinformatics.com/timss/pop1/mpop1.htm, http://timss.bc.edu/timss1995i/TIMSSPDF/BSItems.pdf/, and http://www.ed.gov/inits/Math/timss4_8.html.

———. 2007. *TIMSS 2003, Science Items, Released Set. Fourth Grade.* S011026. Chestnut Hill, Mass.: TIMSS & PIRLS International Study Center, Boston College. timss.bc.edu/PDF/T03_RELEASED_S4.pdf.

Kirsch, I. 2001. *The International Adult Literacy Survey (IALS): Understanding What Was Measured.* Research Report RR-01-25. Princeton, NJ: Educational Testing Service.

Kubiszyn, T., and G. Borich. 2000. *Educational Testing and Measurement.* New York: Wiley.

Linn, R. L., and S. B. Dunbar. 1992. "Issues in the Design and Reporting of the National Assessment of Educational Progress." *Journal of Educational Measurement* 29 (2): 177–94.

Linn, R. L., and M. D. Miller. 2004. *Measurement and Assessment in Teaching: Student Exercise Manual.* Upper Saddle River, NJ: Prentice Hall.

Messick, S. 1987. "Large-Scale Educational Assessment as Policy Research: Aspirations and Limitations." *European Journal of Psychology and Education* 2 (2): 157–65.

———. 1989. "Validity." In *Educational Measurement*, 3rd ed., ed. R. L. Linn, 13–103. New York: American Council on Education/Macmillan.

Mullis, I. V. S, A. M. Kennedy, M. O. Martin, and M. Sainsbury. 2006. *Assessment Framework and Specifications: Progress in International Reading Literacy Study.* 2nd ed. Chestnut Hill, MA: TIMSS and PIRLS International Study Center, Boston College.

Mullis, I. V. S., M. O. Martin, E. J. Gonzalez, and S. J. Chrostowski. 2004. *TIMSS 2003 International Mathematics Report: Findings from IEA's Trends in International Mathematics and Science Study at the Fourth and Eighth Grades.* Chestnut Hill, MA: TIMSS and PIRLS International Study Center, Boston College.

Mullis, I. V. S., M. O. Martin, E. J. Gonzalez, K. D. Gregory, R. A. Garden, K. M. O'Connor, S. J. Chrostowski, and T. A. Smith. 2000. *TIMSS 1999 International Mathematics Report. Findings from IEA's Repeat of the Third International Mathematics and Science Study* at the Eighth Grade. Chestnut Hill, Mass.: The International Study Center, Boston College. timssandpirls. bc.edu/timss1999i/pdf/T99i_Math_2.pdf.

National Assessment Governing Board. No date. *Writing Framework and Specifications for the 1998 National Assessment of Educational Progress.* Washington, DC: U.S. Department of Education.

New Zealand Ministry of Education. 2002. *English in the New Zealand Curriculum.* Wellington: Learning Media for the New Zealand Ministry of Education.

Nitko, A. J. 2004. *Educational Assessment of Students.* 4th ed. Upper Saddle River, NJ: Pearson, Merrill, Prentice Hall.

Papua New Guinea Department of Education. 2003. *Cultural Mathematics Elementary Syllabus.* Port Moresby: Papua New Guinea Department of Education.

———. 2004. *National Curriculum Standards Monitoring Test.* Port Moresby: Papua New Guinea Department of Education.

Philippine Department of Education. 2004. *Region-wide Assessment for Mathematics, Science, and English (RAMSE): Basic Education Assistance for Mindanao (BEAM).* Manila: Philippine Department of Education.

PISA (Programme for International Student Assessment). 2004. *Learning for Tomorrow's World: First Results from PISA 200.* Paris: Organisation for Economic Co-operation and Development.

APPENDIX C

EXAMPLES OF TEST AND QUESTIONNAIRE ITEMS AND ADMINISTRATION MANUALS ON CD

The compact disc (CD) that accompanies this book contains examples of achievement test items, scoring guides, questionnaire items, and manuals that have been used in a variety of contexts, including national and international assessments. Figure C.1 depicts the layout of the CD. Most of the items, questionnaires, and manuals have been made publicly available and can be accessed on the Internet. They are reproduced on a CD to assist assessment teams in some countries where Internet access may be difficult. We gratefully acknowledge the support of the publishers and organizations that gave permission to reproduce their original materials on this CD. They are listed at the end of this appendix.

The examples on the CD can give national assessment teams ideas on item type and format, scoring guides, curriculum content coverage, test and questionnaire layout, and type of information published in test administration manuals. National assessment teams might use this information to help design their own test instruments, scoring guides, and manuals. National assessment teams should keep in mind national curricula and appropriateness of vocabulary and test formats when selecting or adapting material.

FIGURE C.1

Guide to CD Materials on Tests, Questionnaires, and Manuals

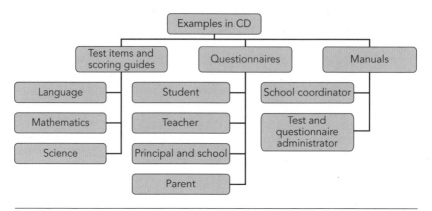

Note: Click on the file "Sources" to access the source of individual released items, questions, or manuals, as well as a list of Web site addresses (where available) from which the released information was obtained.

ACHIEVEMENT TEST ITEMS

The CD contains test items in mathematics, language, and science. We hope that item writers in mathematics, language, and science will find these items useful as they develop assessment instruments based on their own national curricula. It is not the intention that national assessment teams should copy these items. Within each subject, item files for primary-level grades are presented first, followed by postprimary-level item files, followed in turn by item files that cover both primary and postprimary levels.

The CD includes a large collection of items from separate U.S. national studies in mathematics, reading, science, and writing for grades 4, 8, and 12 and from separate studies for ages 9, 13, and 17. It also contains items from grade 4 mathematics Massachusetts state tests. Items used in national studies in Australia and Ireland are also included.

The CD also features released items from three international assessments: Trends in International Mathematics and Science Study (TIMSS) (mathematics and science, for grades 3, 4, 7, 8, and the final year of postprimary school); Progress in International Reading Literacy Study (PIRLS) (language, for grade 4); and Programme for International Student Assessment (PISA) (language, mathematics, and science, for 15-year-olds).

Some of the language-related items apply to extensive passages of text, a format that may not be appropriate in some national assessments. In a number of instances, the format of the downloaded item differs from the format used in the original test booklet. Note that some test items were designed to test two or more grade levels.

The material covered in the CD also includes scoring guides linked with specific tests.

QUESTIONNAIRES

The CD contains separate sample questionnaires for students, teachers, schools and principals, and parents. Most of the questionnaires have been used in international studies in industrial countries. Many of the questions are specific to particular educational and school contexts. National assessment teams should consider adapting some of the more relevant questions to reflect the economic, social, and school realities of their countries.

MANUALS

The CD includes manuals that give specific instructions on how to administer tests and questionnaires. It also includes manuals that outline the roles and responsibilities of those responsible for coordinating the assessment within the schools. These responsibilities include tasks to be undertaken before, during, and after test and questionnaire administration. The examples cover topics such as preparing the test administrators; listing appropriate supplies and materials (such as tests, questionnaires, pencils, and a watch or clock); using seating arrangements to minimize the possibility of copying; dealing with sample items; implementing time guidelines; and identifying tasks that the administrator should complete at the end of each session.

Some of the material will be more relevant in some countries than in others. Some manuals, for instance, refer to machine-scored tests or answer sheets, which tend not to be used in national assessments in many developing countries. Users are cautioned not to try to replicate the contents of the manuals but to select ideas that are most relevant to their particular national contexts. The samples are included to help national assessment teams develop manuals based on their own tests. Some manuals contain suggestions on selecting samples of students within schools.

ACKNOWLEDGMENTS

The National Center for Education Statistics of the U.S. Department of Education (http://nces.ed.gov/nationsreportcard/about) has granted permission to reproduce released test items, test administrators' manuals, and questionnaires from the National Assessment of Educational Progress.

The International Association for the Evaluation of Educational Achievement (http://www.iea.nl/ and http://timss.bc.edu/) has given permission to reproduce released TIMSS and PIRLS items, questionnaires, and school coordinators' and test administrators' manuals.

The Organisation for Economic Co-operation and Development (http://www.pisa.oecd.org/dataoecd/51/27/37474503.pdf) has given permission to reproduce released PISA test items, questionnaires, and school coordinators' and test administrators' manuals.

The CD contains mathematics items that have been released to the public by the Massachusetts Department of Education and that are available on the department's Web site at http://www.doe.mass.edu/mcas/testitems.html.

The Australian Council for Educational Research has granted permission to reproduce sample items and scoring or marking guides from its Literacy and Numeracy National Assessment, Reading, Years 3, 5, and 7 (http://www.acer.edu.au/lanna/).

The Educational Research Centre, Dublin (http://www.erc.ie/index.php?s=7), has granted permission to reproduce English and mathematics items, a questionnaire, and a test administrators' manual.

The CD contains a file that lists the source of individual released items, questions, or manuals, as well as a list of Web site addresses (where available) from which the released information was obtained. Click on the file "Sources" on the CD to access the source of individual released items, questions, or manuals, as well as a list of Web site addresses (where available) from which the released information was obtained.

INDEX

Boxes, figures, notes, and tables are indicated by b, f, n, and t respectively.

absence of student during test, 141
achievement test items, 158–159
administration manual. *See* manual for test administrator
administrators. *See* test administrators
advanced student performance, 25
aggregated variable, 107, 108, 111, 147
alphabetical codes for questionnaire responses, 121
ambiguous responses to questionnaires, 123–124
analysis, 4f
answer sheet, 88, 147, 160
assessment framework
   contexts, 10, 11b, 25–26
   development, 9–26
   framework, definition of, 149
   language of test, 16–17
   overview of, 9–10
   reporting results, 24–25
   stages in test development and questionnaire design, 6–7t, 8
   student population for assessment, 24
   test blueprint or table of specifications, 10–16
   validity and, 16
   See also blueprints; format of items
Australia, 158

basic student performance, 25
below basic student performance, 25
bias of items, 30

blueprints
   for questionnaires, 101t, 102, 105, 106b
   for tests, 6t, 10–16, 13t, 14t, 5f, 28, 55–56, 79, 147

CD material, 8, 157–161
   administration manuals, 129, 142, 159–160
   features of, 8, 158f
   high-quality item samples, 28
   questionnaires, 120, 159
   short-item response item examples, 38
census collectors as test administrators, 139
checklists
   for pretests, 69
   for test administrators, 142, 143–144b
chief rater, 92, 147–148
circular linking, 64–65, 65f, 148
classical item analysis, 148
classical test theory (CTT), 76, 84n
closed constructed-response items
   definition of, 148
   hand scoring of, 21, 23t
   item format, 17–18, 19b, 20–22, 23t, 33, 41b, 44b
   pretest scoring of, 74
   reliability of, 77
cognitive processes, 12, 24, 29
compact disc material. *See* CD material
contextual information, 25–26
costs
   of data processing of questionnaires, 119
   of hand-scoring test items, 20, 21, 22, 23t

of pretest reprinting, 70
of printing, 47, 89
of questionnaire administration, 110
of translated tests, 16, 17
country-specific questionnaire items, 108
cover page information, 68, 85–86, 86*b*, 110
cross-check rating, 21, 148
CTT. *See* classical test theory
curriculum and national assessment, 4*f*, 5*f*, 10, 11*b*

data, definition of, 148
data analysis, 5*f*, 7*t*, 48
    plan for questionnaires, 100, 111
    pretest, 83
data analysis
    software scoring multiple-choice tests, 21
data analyst, 7*t*, 148
data entry sheet, 73–74, 73*b*
definitions
    glossary, 147–152
    of key subject areas, 9–10
design of items, 46–51
    See also layout and design of items
dichotomous score, 80–81, 148
difficulty of items, 15, 29–30, 82, 87
discrepancy rating, 148
discriminating items, 148
discrimination index, 79, 80–81, 81*t*
distractors in multiple-choice test items, 34, 36–38, 148
double-rating, 22, 148

East Timor, 139
electronic storage of test items, 60
essay or extended-response items, 17, 19, 20*b*, 21, 23*t*, 94, 148
external administrators, 139, 146

feedback from respondents on questionnaires, 119–120
field test, 148
    See also pretesting items
final test
    definition of final form, 149
    design of final test, 85–88
    production, 85–90, 88*b*
    printing and proofreading of, 88–90
    selection of test items and, 82–84
flowchart of national assessment activities, 4, 5*f*
font size. *See* layout and design of items
forced-choice responses to questionnaires, 108, 109

format of items
    CD material on, 28
    pretests, 71, 71*b*
    questionnaires, 108–109
    tests, 17–24, 28, 33–46
    See also item writing; closed constructed-response items; essay or extended-response items; multiple-choice items; open-ended items; short-response items
framework, 6*t*, 149
front page of pretest booklets, 68–69
full cohort, 149

glossary, 147–152
graphic design and test items, 47–51, 48*b*, 49*b*, 50*b*
graphs, use of, 47, 49*b*
grayscale
    definition of, 149
    for labels, 47, 59, 67, 88
    questionnaire responses and, 121, 122*b*
    scoring options in, 69

hand-scoring
    advantages and disadvantages of, 22, 23*t*
    of closed constructed-response items, 21, 23*t*
    cost of, 20, 21, 22, 23*t*
    cross-check rating and, 21, 148
    definition of, 149
    guides for, 21–22, 73–75, 82, 85, 91, 93–94
    of multiple-choice items, 21
    of open-ended short-response items, 21, 23*t*
    of pretests, 72, 74, 75
    of questionnaires, 108
    raters and, 92–95
    tasks, 6*t*, 7*t*
head teacher, 104–105, 126, 131–132
history of developed test items, importance of saving, 59
home factors, 26
horizontal linking, 87, 149

ID numbers for students, 86, 126
illness of student during test, 141
images in test items, 47–51, 51*b*
implementing agency, 4*f*, 5*f*, 6*t*, 7*t*
incorrect response, 93, 149
informing schools about national assessment, 145–146
instructions
    for students, 129, 131, 133, 134
    for test administrator, 133*b*, 140–142

International Literacy Survey, 24–25
Internet availability of test items, 28
Ireland, 24, 158
IRT. *See* item response theory
item, definition of, 149
item classifications, 59, 60, 83
item format. *See* format of items
item labels, 47, 58–59, 63, 88
item layout and design, 46–49
item panels, 46, 55–57, 74–75, 149
item pool, 14*t*, 57, 59, 149
item pre-testing, 61–77
item response modeling, 25
item response theory (IRT), 76, 84*n*
item selection. *See* selection of test items
item style sheet, 54*b*
item writing
   characteristics of good items, 27–28
   difficulty of items, 15, 29–30, 87
   format of items, 17–24, 33–46
   item bias, 30
   item panels, 5*f*, 46, 55–57, 74–75, 149
   item-writing team, 52–55, 54*b*, 83
   models of high-quality items, 28
   practice items, 45–46
   for questionnaires, 101*t*, 113–120
   reference groups and, 57–58
   reviewers, other, 57–58
   samples of high-quality items, 28
   stimulus material, 30–32, 32*b*, 33*b*, 51*b*,
     68, 87, 151
   tasks, 6*t*, 7*t*
   topics, 27–60
   team for, 52–55, 54*b*, 83
   tracking items, 58–60
   writers, qualities and training of, 52–55
   See also layout and design of items

key in multiple-choice test items, 34,
   37–38, 83, 150

labeling test forms, 63
language of tests and questionnaires,
   16–17, 109
language test, 94
layout and design of items
   advantages and disadvantages of, 22, 23*t*
   basic guidelines, 46–47
   closed constructed-response items.
     See closed constructed-response items
   essay or extended-response items.
     See essay or extended-response items
   final test production, 87, 88
   grayscale, use of. *See* grayscale
   multiple-choice items. *See* multiple-
     choice items

open-ended short response items.
     See open-ended short response items
partial-credit items, 41–44, 42*b*, 43*b*,
   44*b*, 74
pretests, 69, 71, 71*b*
quality of images, 9, 47–51, 48*b*, 49*b*,
   50*b*, 51*b*
questionnaires, 117–118, 118*b*
short-response items. *See* short-response
   items
student responses, 88
style sheet for writers, 54–55
topics, 46–51
units, 44–45, 152
leading raters, 92, 149
learning areas, 10, 27, 52, 149
learning outcomes, 29
length of test booklets, 88–89
letters of endorsement for external
   administrators, 146
linear linking, 65, 149
linked items and forms, 63–67, 65*f*, 66*f*,
   67*t*, 83, 87, 149
logistics, 4*f*
longitudinal linking, 150

manual for test administrator
   CD inclusion of, 129, 142, 159–160
   contents of, 130–131
   definition of, 147
   features of, 132, 133*b*
   instructions for, 133*b*, 140–142
   necessary details in, 132–134, 134*b*
   overview, 129
   practice questions, 134, 135,
     135*b*, 136*b*
   review of, 137
   student instructions, 129, 131, 133, 134
   topics, 129–137
   tryout for, 134, 136
   use of, 131–132
maps, use of, 47, 50*b*
Massachusetts, 158
matching questionnaires and test data,
   125–126
materials allowed during testing, 141
ministry of education (MOE), 3, 5*f*
missing scores or responses, 41, 72–73,
   123–124, 150
multiple booklets, procedure for
   use, 87
multiple-choice items
   definition of, 17–18
   item format, 17–18, 20–22, 23*t*,
     29–30, 34–38, 34*b*, 35*b*, 36*b*, 37*b*
   in questionnaires, 121–123, 124

scoring guides, 73–74
  test item selection and, 79–80, 81*t*
multiple possible questionnaire responses,
  121–123, 122*b*

NAEP. *See* U.S. National Assessment of
  Educational Progress
national assessment activities
  flowchart of, 4, 5*f*
  overview of, 4, 5–7*f*
National Assessment of English Reading
  (Ireland), 24
national identification numbers for
  students, 86
national steering committee (NSC), 3, 4*f*,
  5*f*, 6*t*, 9, 25
New Zealand, 11*b*
no-attempt scores, 72
numerical codes for questionnaire
  responses, 121
numerical identity (ID) for students,
  86, 126

objectivity, 151
open-ended short response items
  definition of, 150
  item format, 17, 19–22, 23*t*, 33,
    38–40, 42–43, 43*b*
  pretests, scoring of, 74
  questionnaires and, 108, 120
  reliability and, 77
  scoring guides, 41–44
  test item selection and, 80–82, 81*t*
oral administration of tests, 17

panels
  item, 5*f*, 46, 55–57, 74–75, 149
  for questionnaire reviews, 119
Papua New Guinea
  blueprint for mathematics content in,
    14, 15*f*
  mathematics curriculum in, 11*b*
  mathematics tests in, 22, 24*t*
  questionnaire blueprint in, 105, 106*b*
parent questionnaires, 103, 126
partial-credit items
  definition of, 150
  item format and, 33
  pretests, 75
  scoring guides for, 41–44, 42*b*, 43*b*,
    44*b*, 74
  selection of test items and, 81–82, 81*t*
percentage of test item types, 20
Philippines, 142, 143–144*b*
pictures, use of, 48*b*

pilot test, 150
  See also pretesting items
PIRLS. *See* Progress in International
  Reading Literacy Study
PISA. *See* Programme for International
  Student Assessment
point-biserial correlation, 79–82, 80*t*,
  82*t*, 150
policy makers
  assessment framework development and,
    10, 14, 15, 25–26
  definition of, 150
  item panels and, 56
  national assessment stages in test
    development and questionnaire design
    and, 6*t*
  questionnaires and, 99–100, 101*t*, 102,
    105, 106*b*, 107, 110, 117, 119
pool of items. *See* item pool
practice items, 45–46, 135, 137
  in questionnaires, 134
practice questions, 134, 135–136*b*
preset standards for tests, 16
pretesting items
  data entry sheet for, 73–74, 73*b*
  definition of pretest, 150
  design of pretest form, 64–68, 65*f*, 66*f*,
    67*t*, 68*t*
  difficulty of items and, 29, 82
  failure to attempt test items, 72
  field test and, 148
  final test data and, 82–83
  implementation of pretest, 70–71, 71*b*
  manual for test administrator and, 134,
    136–137
  model and sample tests and, 28
  overview, 61–64
  printing and proofreading of pretest,
    68–70, 90
  reliability and, 76–77
  scoring pretest, 71–78, 73*b*
  suitability of items and, 15
  tasks, 5*f*
  topics, 61–67
  tracking items and, 58
  trial test and, 152
principals
  administrators' manual for, 131–132
  national assessment, informing of,
    145–146
printing and proofreading, 6*t*, 7*t*
  definition of proofreading, 150
  of final test, 88–90
  of pretest, 68–70
  of test administrators' manual, 137

proficiency levels, 25
proficient student performance, 25
Programme for International Student
    Assessment (PISA), 19, 28, 38, 159
Progress in International Reading Literacy
    Study (PIRLS), 19, 25, 28, 38, 45, 159
proofreading. *See* printing and proofreading
publicly released test items, 28
punctuation in item writing, 35, 47

quality assurance, 72, 142
questionnaires
    administration of, 110
    blueprint for, 101*t*, 102, 105, 106*b*
    CD material on, 120, 159
    coding responses, 121–124, 122*b*, 150
    components in development of, 100, 101*t*
    construction, 97–111
    content of, 102–105
    contextual information, obtaining, 26
    data analysis plan, 101*t*, 111
    data entry, 123
    design of, 6–7*t*, 8, 99–111, 101*t*
    final, 101*t*
    item format, 107*t*, 108–109
    item writing for, 101*t*, 113–120, 118*b*
    language of, 109
    layout, 117–118, 118*b*
    matching with test data, 125–126
    pretest, 101*t*
    questions, 114
    respondents of, 109–110
    response categories, 115–117
    review of, 119–120
    sensitive issues, 117
    statements, 114–115
    steps in development of, 100

random sample, 62, 150
raters and hand-scoring of test items,
    92–95, 150
rating center, 91, 92
raw variable, 107, 108
reference group, review by, 57–58
reliability, 76–77, 79, 151
reporting results, 24–25
respondents of questionnaires, 109–110
responses to questionnaires, 122*b*
results, reporting of, 24–25
review and reviewers, 46, 55–58, 74–75,
    119–120, 137, 149
rotated booklet design, 62

scanning, use of, 21
school factors, 26

school inspectors as test administrators,
    139
scoring
    definition of score, 151
    guides, 21–22, 38, 41, 54–55, 54*b*, 60,
        73–74, 151
    missing scores or responses, 41, 72–73,
        123–124, 150
    of multiple-choice items, 73–74
    of partial-credit items, 41–44, 42*b*, 43*b*,
        44*b*, 74, 75
    of pretests, 71–78, 73*b*, 75
    See also hand-scoring; *specific test items*
secure items, 28, 151
secure storage of test materials, 60, 132,
    133*b*, 144*b*
selected readings, 153–155
selection of test items, 79–84, 80*t*, 81*t*
sensitive issues in item writing, 117
short-response items
    hand-scoring of, 94
    item format, 17–19, 33–34, 38–41,
        40*b*, 41
    partial-credit items and, 41–44, 42*b*,
        43*b*, 44*b*
    practice items and, 45
single common set of link items, 64
socioeconomic background data, 26*n*
software, 58–59, 74
spreadsheet use, 59–60, 67–68, 68*t*
stages in test development and question-
    naire design, 6–7*t*
standardized conditions, 139, 151
statistical requirements of final test, 85
stem in multiple-choice test items, 34–35,
    36, 44, 151
stimulus material, 30–32, 32*b*, 33*b*, 51*b*,
    68, 87, 151
student background information,
    85–87, 109
students
    motivation of, 145
    population for assessment, 24
    questionnaires for, 103, 125–126
style sheet for item writers, 54–55
subject specialists, 4*f*, 5*f*, 6*t*, 12
substrand, 14, 151
summaries of questionnaire data, 109
supervision of test administrators, 142

table of specifications, 10–16
    See also blueprints
teachers
    national assessment, informing of,
        145–146

questionnaires for, 104, 126
as test administrators, 140, 142
team for item writing, 52–55, 54b, 83
team leader, 5f, 6t
test, defined, 151
test administrators
    checklist for, 142, 143–144b
    choice of, 139–140
    definition of, 147
    instructions for, 133b, 140–142
    quality assurance, 142
    single vs. multiple booklet use
        and, 87
    tasks, 5f, 6t
    topics, 139–144
    See also manual for test administrator
test blueprints. *See* blueprints
test data and questionnaires, matching of,
    125–126
test development manager
    quality control by, 72
    questionnaire content and, 102
    rater training, 92
    responsibilities, 55, 57
    tasks, 4f, 7t
    test administrators' manual and, 137
    tracking items, 59
test objectivity, 151
test population, 24, 56, 67, 151
test usefulness, 70, 74, 151
text type, 28
    See also layout and design of items

Third International Mathematics
    and Science Study (TIMSS),
    12, 14t
time allowed for test taking, 22, 63, 141
TIMSS. *See* Third International Mathematics
    and Science Study; Trends in
    International Mathematics and Science
    Study
tracking items, 58–60
training
    of item writers, 53–55, 54b, 55
    of raters, 92–94
    for test administrators, 142
translation of tests, 16–17
Trends in International Mathematics and
    Science Study (TIMSS), 26n, 28,
    116–117, 158–159
trial test, 152
    See also pretesting items

unbiased items, 57, 152
units, writing items for, 44–45, 152
U.S. National Assessment of
    Educational Progress (NAEP),
    28, 60n
usefulness of test. *See* test usefulness

validity, 16, 151
vertical linking, 65–66, 66f, 87, 152

writers of test items, qualities and training
    of, 52–55, 54b, 74–75

ECO-AUDIT
Environmental Benefits Statement

The World Bank is committed to preserving endangered forests and natural resources. The Office of the Publisher has chosen to print *Developing Tests and Questionnaires for a National Assessment of Educational Achievement* on recycled paper with 30 percent post-consumer waste, in accordance with the recommended standards for paper usage set by the Green Press Initiative, a nonprofit program supporting publishers in using fiber that is not sourced from endangered forests. For more information, visit www.greenpressinitiative.org.

Saved:
• 8 trees
• 6 million BTUs less used
• 746 lbs CO_2 less released into the atmosphere
• 3,098 gallons less of water used
• 2,291 pounds less of waste generated